COLLINS FIELD GUIDE

Fields

COLLINS FIELD GUIDE

Fields

by BILL LAWS

Collins

ACKNOWLEDGEMENTS

I am grateful to Edward Abell, Hugh Bryant, Alison Chapman, Stuart Chatfield, Abby Laws, Paige Mitchell, Mike Jackson, Lillian Smith and Cecile Egan for their assistance; to Ali Burns for permission to quote from her song 'Fenland'; to library staff at Holme Lacy College of Agriculture; to Sarah Laws and Rob Watkins for their research, to Sandy Green for her diligent editing, and to my agent, Chelsey Fox, for her support.

Contents

An Introduction to Fields

From the rice paddies of Asia to the buttercup-filled water meadows of Europe, and from the lush green paddocks of New Zealand to the wide-open plains of the American Midwest, the field is the face of the countryside.

Two billion people labour in the field today, yet the field fascinates us all. Beethoven wrote his *Pastoral Symphony* to evoke its rural idyll, while the roots of popular music can be traced back to the work songs of the field. Writers and artists including Virgil, William Shakespeare, John Constable, Alfred, Lord Tennyson, William Blake, Vincent van Gogh, Henry Thoreau, Raoul Dufy, Grant Wood and Andrew Wyeth have all been inspired by the field. When the Impressionist painter Claude Monet was asked about his studio he gestured at the fields of northern France and declared, 'That is my studio.'

The birth of civilisation was triggered by the founding of fields. Long ago, and in different parts of the world, people stopped hunting and, instead, started hacking at the wilderness with stone blades and axes. They enclosed grasslands with thorn-bush fences and drove half-domesticated beasts to be pastured in paddocks. When the time came, the animals were slaughtered, with due thanks and ceremony, and the meat preserved for the winter ahead.

Stones were cleared from arable ground and banked into boundaries. Within them the virgin soil was turned and the seeds of the future sown, once again with due ceremony. When the harvest moon had crested the horizon and the crop was safely gathered, the harvest celebrations could begin. For more than 10,000 years this cycle, sowing, growing, harvesting and celebrating, has continued.

Why the fields began in the first place is a real mystery. Archaeologists have uncovered many of the first fields. They have discovered which crops and animals were raised and can shed light on the early farming methods. Yet they can find no clear explanation as to why fields were founded, in places as far apart as the Middle East and South America, and all around the same time.

Today nearly 40 per cent of Earth's land has been put to the plough, a process that has shaped the landscape in which we live. Fly over virtually any part of the world and the view below is patterned by the patchwork of fields: tea plantations curl around a Sri Lankan hillside like chunky, green knitwear; in the American Midwest the golden sweep of prairie wheat fields edges up to a cluster of farmyard grain silos; elsewhere, on the high plains of Andalusia, olive groves pepper the sun-burned sierra.

In its 10,000 years of history the field has tamed the wilderness, fashioned the landscape and become a tool for social change, both good and bad. The English Enclosures transformed the open fields of the Midland shires, altering them into what the poet John Clare claimed was 'a curse upon the land'; the 19th-century cotton fields of the Americas enslaved a whole race of black African slaves; and millions starved when Stalin set about the collectivisation of the fields in the former Soviet Union.

Millions more would have died from starvation but for the great field crop, grain. 'Who sows wheat, sows God', declared the Greeks, acknowledging grain's two most important assets: its nutrients and its suitability for storage. Grain has even changed the shape of the human face, the jaw line shifting from the edge-to-edge set of the carnivore to the grinding 'overbite' of the grain-eater.

The sowing, growing and harvesting of the three most significant grains, wheat, rice and maize (corn), lay behind the founding of great empires in China, South America, the Mediterranean, Europe and, most recently, America. Each shift of global power was accompanied by the extension of the fields' reign and the development of ever more sophisticated tools and technologies. The roots of modern technology lie not in the lab but in the field. However, there has been an environmental downside. Mechanisation, pesticides, fertilisers and habitat destruction have severed vital links in the wildlife chain: birds and beasts that once called from the field margins have slipped into oblivion; the poet Edmund Spenser's 'pink and purple columbine, gillyflowers, daffadowndillies, cowslips, kingcups, and loved Lilies' are in retreat. A great deal of controversy continues to surround issues such as genetically modified foods, the growing of biofuels, and the unsustainable use of fossil fuels to cultivate the world's fields.

Meanwhile, slash-and-burn farming is causing the world's rainforests to disappear at an alarming rate, displacing indigenous people and annihilating many potentially useful plants and insects before they have even been recorded.

Establishing a balance between the wild world and the field is crucial to our life on Earth. If the wilderness is destroyed we face environmental collapse. If the fields were to fail, we would starve in a matter of months.

Chapter One

FIELD
FOREBEARS

When was the first field created, and where? Was it originated by Egyptians, Native Americans, Chinese or Europeans? What did it look like? And what did it grow: maize (corn), wheat or rice? The origin of the first field is tied to a curious and unexplained event: the birth of agriculture around 12,000 years ago. Fields in myriad forms have been with us for that long, and who knows where the fields of the future will take us?

The Birth of Civilisation

According to scholars such as Jared Diamond, the birth of agriculture brought with it nothing less than the birth of civilisation – an idea that forms a key part of his Pulitzer-Prize–winning book *Guns, Germs and Steel*. Today, 37 per cent of Earth's land is devoted to fields of pasture and crops. It is not enough. According to UNESCO, 25,000 people die of hunger every day. If field-based agriculture suddenly ceased, humanity would be facing starvation within about two months as world food stocks ran out. As these stark figures illustrate, fields are the building blocks of human life. They are the places where we grow plants programmed to that remarkable equation: $6H_2O + 6CO_2 + light \rightarrow C_6H_{12}O_6 + 6O_2$. Or, if you prefer, the conversion of carbon dioxide, water and light into sugars, or carbohydrates, and oxygen. This is photosynthesis, the almost miraculous process where plant chlorophyll, powered by the sun, turns carbon dioxide and water into edible sugars. This process sustains life on our planet. Without plants – and the fields where they grow – life would cease.

Unlike us, the earliest members of the human race, who sought out and chased down their food somewhere in southern Africa several million years ago, needed no fields. It was not until the retreat of ice sheets covering millions of square miles of land in the Northern Hemisphere that the first hedge banks and thorn fences appeared. They arose in the semi-arid Middle East. The year was around 10,000 B.C.E.

A scene from the distant past or an example of present-day farming in a developing region of the globe? In some parts of the world, fields are little changed from their ancient ancestors.

Perhaps a thousand years later (a brief moment in prehistory), hunter-gatherers in other parts of the world began fielding their food: near the Yangtze River in South China, the Yellow River in North China, sub-Saharan Africa, the South American Andes, central Mexico and eastern parts of North America. The world's first agricultural revolution had begun.

A Brief History of Agriculture

Imagine the last 12 millennia compressed into the 12 months of a calendar year. French and Spanish hunters finished daubing their cave walls with accounts of the hunt at Lascaux and Altamira in December of the previous year; now, in January of the new year, people are gathering wild cereals. A month later they are taming wild sheep and goats, and sowing emmer and einkorn, the predecessors of our modern wheat, in newly established fields. By March they are domesticating wild cattle and pigs, and making the most of the creatures' milk, meat and hides.

By this time that most serviceable of animals, the pig, has been brought under domestication in China. And by April (or from 7000 B.C.E.) people are growing fields of beans and squash on the other side of the world in Peru. Field crops are growing in New Guinea, Greece and the Balkans. Farming is spreading across the globe.

By May, the northeast of the Indian subcontinent has started farming. Farmers are growing millet and broomcorn in northern China, rice in southern China, and wheat and barley in Egypt. There are crops of bulrush millet ripening in the Sahara, even as the desert creeps up on the crops; while in Spain, central Europe and eastern America, hunter-gatherer tribes are giving up on the chase in favour of more permanent settlements.

By June, zebu cattle, still traded in Madagascar, are fattening in Pakistan; donkeys have been tamed in Egypt, horses in Ukraine, and llamas and alpacas in Peru. Ox-drawn ploughs are breaking fresh soil in the Balkans; the Sudanese are sowing their first crops of sorghum and rice; and the fashion for farming has reached as far into Europe as the Netherlands. Olives, figs, almonds and pomegranates are being cultivated on the eastern banks of the Mediterranean, along with the all-important maize and cotton in Mexico.

Work starts on Britain's Stonehenge in July, long after most of the island's thick blanket of forest has been felled. Farmers are putting down roots in southern Sweden, and in Mesopotamia Sumerians are converting their pulling sleds into farm carts thanks to a new invention: the wheel.

As we reach August (or 5,000 years ago), the Indus Valley civilisation is emerging in modern-day Pakistan. In Malaysia, farmers are growing breadfruit; in Peru, chilies, avocados, groundnuts, potatoes and sweet potatoes; and in North America, sunflowers, sump weed, goose grass and squashes. As the bull dancers of the Minoan civilisation practise their art on the island of Crete, pyramids are being planned in Egypt and menhirs (standing stones) are being erected in Brittany in northwest France. In Ireland, they are laying stone walls around their fields (see Europe's Oldest Fields, page 25).

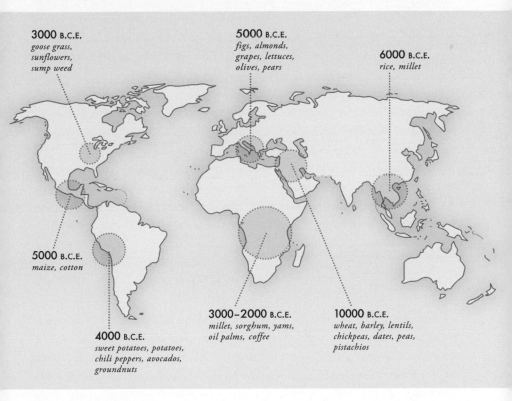

3000 B.C.E.
goose grass,
sunflowers,
sump weed

5000 B.C.E.
figs, almonds,
grapes, lettuces,
olives, pears

6000 B.C.E.
rice, millet

5000 B.C.E.
maize, cotton

4000 B.C.E.
sweet potatoes, potatoes,
chili peppers, avocados,
groundnuts

3000–2000 B.C.E.
millet, sorghum, yams,
oil palms, coffee

10000 B.C.E.
wheat, barley, lentils,
chickpeas, dates, peas,
pistachios

The domestication of crops was a truly global event, occurring spontaneously and largely independently in different regions at different times. Inevitably, this is a reflection of local variations, such as the presence of different wild species and the ease with which they could be grown. For more, see Chapter Four: Field Flora

By autumn, a succession of mighty civilisations – the Phoenicians, Mycenaeans, Egyptians, Maya and Greeks – have risen and fallen. Knotweed, little barley and maygrass are brought into the kitchen in eastern America, while, according to Homer, 'fruits, also sweet figs and bounteous olives' are growing in his native Greece. By 300 B.C.E., celery, beets, carrots, cabbages and asparagus are being raised all around the southern Mediterranean, along with peas, vetch, wheat and barley in northern Europe.

As we reach November, the last great superpower before those of the 20th century, Rome, is marching on Gaul (now France), Caesar's legionnaires bringing their own garlic, onions, leeks, lettuces, parsnips and turnips to feed the campaign. However, just two weeks later on our timescale, the western Roman Empire comes to an end, and it is the turn of the religious foundations – Christian, Buddhist and Islamic – to foster the field. In early December, the last of Spain's Moorish leaders, Muhammad XII, known as Boabdil to the Spanish, surrenders the keys of Granada to his Christian conquerors, leaving the *huertas verduras* (the 'irrigated lands') behind. Hectares of vegetables still grow there, in Valencia, under the gaze of derelict Moorish castles.

By mid-December, when Sir Francis Drake claims what is now California for Queen Elizabeth I of England, a second agricultural revolution is approaching: the two-way trade in plants between America and Europe. Then, in 1850, or shortly after 25 December, more than a million Europeans die of starvation. The Irish potato fields have failed. Thus, within the space of 12 months – or 12,000 years – most of the world has settled into the agricultural life. Mistakes in the field are already being made.

The First Kingdom

Mesopotamia formed one blade of the Fertile Crescent – that once-rich, boomerang-shaped piece of land that lay across the Middle East, its crest in southeast Turkey, its western arm running down through Lebanon and Israel to Jericho and the Dead Sea. In Greek, *Mesopotamia* means 'the land between the rivers'. If the world's first field were to be found anywhere, it would be here, in the semi-arid lands that lay between the Tigris and Euphrates. The sources of these two rivers rose respectively in the snowmelt on the flanks of the Zagros Mountains and in the Armenian cordillera before flowing south through the countryside, the fens of the marsh Arabs, and into the Persian

Gulf. Now buried beneath modern Iraq, northeastern Syria, southeastern Turkey and southwest Iran, Mesopotamia was subjugated by a succession of empires from the Sumerians and Babylonians to the Assyrians and Persians, before converting to Islam in 637 B.C.E. In its 6,000 years of history it witnessed the founding of the world's first cities and the first recorded wars between city-states. In the 20th century, conflict continued to rage in old Mesopotamia, but this time over its oil fields.

After the last ice age, Mesopotamia was chillier and drier than it is today. As the climate warmed, wild grains such as einkorn and emmer (see page 16) started to grow. Hunter-gatherers harvested these species of wild wheat with scythes fashioned from sharpened flints set in animal bones. Although they didn't know it, these stooping families, cutting, gathering and threshing their wild grains, were the world's first farmers. They cropped the fields and supplemented the grain with meat, wild lentils, nuts, hackberries and caper berries. They settled, sowing seed from the last year's crop in fields fenced against the wild; they worked together to bring in the harvest and thresh the corn. When the native goats, rabbits, sheep, deer and the local wild ass, the onager, were caught robbing the crops, the creatures were killed and eaten. In time, the animals were tamed and corralled in new village pastures.

Rival hunter-gatherers who subsisted on the margins of the new communities were driven away, enslaved or persuaded to set up camp themselves as stocks of wild game dwindled. (Hunter-gatherers need thousands of acres to support themselves, while these early farming families could subsist on just 25 acres.) The pool of skills within communities diversified as pot makers and builders, tool makers and weavers withdrew from manual labour to specialise and meet

'Plant and animal domestication is the most important development in the past 13,000 years of human history. It interests all of us ... it was prerequisite to the rise of civilisation and it transformed global demography.'

Jared Diamond writing in *Nature*, 2002

EMMER

Name: Emmer (or farro in Italy)
(*Triticum dicoccon*)

What it's like: Derived from one of civilisation's earliest grains, emmer, like einkorn and spelt wheat, is a primitive version of the wheat we raise today. Grown on a long stem, this is a 'hulled' wheat – that is, one with strong husks enclosing the grain and grown on a branching rachis.

The rachis is brittle and shatters, scattering the seed as soon as it is ripe. This must have made harvesting difficult for early farmers, who would have had to waste time and energy scrabbling in the dirt to collect the grain. Gradually, however, evolution would select strains of emmer that possessed a less brittle rachis. This was a long-drawn-out process, taking up to 1,000 years before a truly cultivatable variety had been selected.

The wild emmer seeds had an extraordinary capacity to self-seed. Once the grain fell, the husks surrounding the seed reacted to warm, humid nights and forced the seed into the soil, the husks twisting like the legs of a frog in a pond. The fine hairs on the husks kept the seed anchored in its new planting place during the day.

Where it's grown: Emmer was widely cultivated in the ancient world and was one of the first crops domesticated in the Middle East. It is far less widespread in modern times, but is still grown in the uplands of Morocco, Spain (Asturias), the Carpathian mountains on the border of the Czech and Slovak republics, and in Albania, Turkey, Switzerland and Italy.

the community's needs. For the community to feel safe they needed to enjoy a surplus of food, and a rat-proof grain store – the world's first farm building – was an early priority.

Villages grew into market towns, market towns into cities. The Sumerians built two of the world's early cities, Uruk and Ur, on the banks of the Euphrates River between 5000 and 4000 B.C.E.; their temple-topped ziggurats (stepped pyramids) gazed out on the irrigated pastures of the south, where goats and cows reared on the riverside pastures kept the populace supplied with meat, milk, butter and skins.

Frieze painters at the temple of Ninhursag, in Tell 'Ubaid, worked like modern-day documentary photographers to record scenes from the cowshed: dairy workers milking cattle, straining milk and churning cream to make butter. Their scribes, employing some of the earliest modes of writing, noted down the food and beer stocks (it was barley that gave the Sumerians the raw ingredients for brewing). And in one 4,500-year-old grave at Ur, a deceased nobleman went to meet his maker in the company of a gold and lapis lazuli representation of the stud goat, the gilded Ram in a Thicket, which had contributed so much to the new economy.

Mesopotamia's nascent fieldwork continued its development under the Egyptians as they laid the foundations for their great civilisation, around five millennia ago, raising their cattle and cultivating their grain on the silt-rich banks of the Nile.

When, in the wake of the Nile's annual inundation, the flood waters receded from the fields, leaving behind a fresh layer of fine soil, the farmers planted their crops, shooed away the birds, and waited. A tomb painting from the time records the result. In the distance, a woman sits collecting fruit from a tree; in the foreground, bent-backed workers stoop to slice a swaying stand of corn with their moon-shaped sickles. One reaper stops to slake his thirst from a clay jar brought to him by a young girl and her brother; and, as pairs of men heave baskets weighed down with corn onto their shoulders, a couple who had been gleaning the dropped grain fall into a fight over the spoils. Later, workmen winnow the corn, throwing it high in the air so that the wind can blow away the chaff. A bevy of clerks kneel with their writing boards to record the size of the harvest.

In an extraordinary chain of events, scenes like these are still being played out in many of the world's fields today, some 5,000 years later. In fact, in some parts of the world, it is as if time has stood still in the field.

The Middle Kingdom

The Middle Kingdom, as the Chinese call their country, is the longest continuous civilisation in history. And with a population of 1.3 billion, the People's Republic of China has the largest agricultural economy in the world. This was one of the first countries to domesticate the pig and – incredibly – it now rears almost half the world's swine, as well as a quarter of its goats.

It started, as it had in Mesopotamia, at the riverside. The first fields were founded on the banks of the Yangtze in southern China and the Yellow River in the north. The flow of the Yangtze is naturally regulated by the Dongting and Poyang lakes, unlike the Yellow River, which earned the soubriquet 'China's Sorrow'. Discoloured by the fine sand, or loess, blown into the waters from the Gobi Desert in the west, the silted Yellow River regularly floods with devastating results. Nevertheless, it was on these riversides that Neolithic tribes cultivated millet and, to the south near the Huai River, rice, around 8,000 years ago. As elsewhere, these were people in transition from hunting and gathering to fully fledged farming: archaeologists sifting through the Neolithic rubbish tips have found the remnants of both domesticated and wild animals in the same pit.

According to Chinese mythology, Shen Nung and Fu His, two of the Five Sovereigns who taught the people everything they needed to know, counselled the first settlers in the art of hunting, fishing and farming. By 221 B.C.E., the First Emperor, Qin Shi Huang, had unified the Chinese Empire. Qin Shi Huang saw to the standardisation of weights, measures and the written word. He began the construction of what would later become the Great Wall of China and achieved a place in posterity (and perhaps the afterlife) by being buried near Lishan (Mount Li), in a vast mausoleum, together with thousands of life-sized terracotta figures with horses.

But it was the Chinese farmers who sustained this empire, paying their taxes in grain, which in turn fed the bureaucratic classes and the army that protected them. It also fuelled stores that were opened at times of famine. The poor peasant farmers even contributed to the construction of the Great Wall, being drafted in when supplies of forced labour from the prisons ran low. When they had worked themselves to death, their bodies were buried in the battlements. It was the farmers, too, who helped build the world's longest canal. No civil-engineering project has taken quite so long to complete: started in 486 B.C.E. and finished over a thousand years later, the 1,800-kilometre (1,115-mile) canal linked the

Yangtze with the Yellow River and helped irrigate the surrounding countryside. 'Dragon bones' found on the banks of the Yellow River, and sold for centuries for their healing powers, were later discovered to be questions inscribed on bone, regarding agricultural matters (and other important issues such as the gender of a forthcoming child) put by the king during the Shang dynasty (1766 to 1059 B.C.E.) to his ancestors. While wheat grown in the north and rice in the south turned into the staple crops that fuelled the nation's growth, the Chinese fields yielded other produce: ginkgo seeds, oranges, chestnuts, walnuts, kiwi fruit, tea (introduced to Europe in the early 17th century and later to America), and the mulberry, on which the silk worm, and the silk industry, depended. There were orchards of plums, too, the early spring blossom signalling personal renewal as well as being a valuable crop.

And so the Chinese peasantry continued tilling the soil, used and all too often abused by their own, and later foreign, rulers. Meanwhile, a crop was growing in neighbouring India, one that would result in the subjugation of the Chinese peasantry, the Chinese Revolution, and the subsequent emergence of the world's largest communist state: *Papaver somniferum,* the opium poppy. (See Opium Fields, pages 71–3.)

Adapting to Change

Pockets of land around the world still support small tribes of hunter-gatherers. In Greenland, the Kalaallit Inuit have survived for centuries along the coast, hunting seals and whales for food and clothing. In Botswana and Namibia, some 30,000 Kung San bushmen battle against drought, cattle herding and government interference to follow their hunting and gathering traditions. In New Guinea, logging and deforestation threaten the hunter-gatherer Amungme tribe, while the spread of wheat fields is putting pressure on the livelihood of the Maasai in central Africa. These are the last of the hunter-gatherers, who have culled and collected their food from the wild for two million years – the resilient remnants left behind when the rest of the world switched from chasing game to taming it around 10,000 years ago.

Early historians conceived the spread of farming as a chain reaction, almost as if a stone had been dropped into the pool of the Fertile Crescent, sending ripples of agricultural knowledge out across the world. Then, archaeological evidence emerged of farmers creating their fields independently of each other and in different parts of the globe. There was China on one side of the world, with its millet and rice, and America on the other, with its maize and beans. Archaeologists began finding field evidence in Africa, India and Central and South Asia. It was almost as if the world had been programmed to adopt the economics of the field at a particular point in its development. It was clearly time to reconsider the evidence.

Perhaps farming was the result of climate change? When the last ice age ended and the snows melted, the resulting flooding was of biblical proportions. Sea levels rose by a dramatic 130 metres (430 feet) in some places and a twentieth of the land slipped below the ocean's surface. Did this precipitate a world-wide crisis that limited the available hunting lands and forced people to start forming fields and settling down to village life? Or was it the result of drought? One theory poses the possibility that, in the post–ice age era, the Fertile Crescent had been subjected to a sustained drought that forced wild animals and people to share the limited resources of the watercourses. In that uneasy coexistence on the river deltas, did people capture and fence in flocks of wild sheep and goats to breed them in captivity?

Perhaps the first field was founded by a tribe of people decimated by starvation? One idea (it remains only a theory) supposes that the first piece of cultivation was precipitated by the world's first famine, triggered by a world population too large to continue feeding itself through hunting and gathering alone. When the first fields were being formed, the world population is estimated to have been between five and ten million. Within 8,000 years it was 30 million. By the 19th-century Industrial Revolution it had reached a billion, and by 2025 it is expected to reach eight billion. Farmers will need to grow almost 30 per cent more grain than they do now to feed everyone.

The roots of this exponential rise in the population can be found in the first days of the field. Had the natural and sustainable balance between hunter-gatherers and the wilderness been reached and passed? Was humankind about to be ejected from the natural Garden of Eden, having exhausted its riches, and would it now be enslaved, tilling the bare earth? These troubles did not end with the loss of the wilderness. Farmers experienced problems with their fields almost as soon as they settled to farm them. There are signs of a serious setback for farming communities in central and eastern Europe around 2700 B.C.E. that could have been caused by an early instance of soil exhaustion. Crops that had shown lusty growth in the new fields soon began to decline. Fields needed rest, needed to lie fallow for a season at least to recover their fertility. ('Fallow', from

MAIZE

Name: Maize, also known as corn
(*Zeu mays*)

What it's like: As the agriculturalist William Cobbett described it in his *Cottage Economy* of 1821: 'The stalks or ears come out of the side of the plant, which has leaves like a flag and which grows to three foot [one metre] high.' He added: 'I, last April, sent parcels of the seed into several countries, to be given away to working men. This corn is the very best for hog-fattening in the whole world.' This tall, swaying member of the grass family goes by a lexicon of names from corn, sweet corn or Indian corn to mealies and maize. The Mexicans called it *cintli* in deference to their goddess of grain, Cintleutl, and grew it in the *milpa* or corn fields. Cuban Indians dubbed it *maisi* (the Spanish *maiz*), the name it retained, somewhat corrupted, when Columbus brought the Cuban plant to Europe in 1573. Within a century, cultivation had reached as far as China. An English author, E. A. Bunyard, recommended adopting 'the principle of the lathe' when eating corn from the cob. Americans did so with enthusiasm (and used the cob as a disposable tobacco pipe). Between 1810 and 1910, the population of the United States rose from 7 million to 92 million, a testament, in part, to the nutritious nature of a maize-fed diet.

Where it's grown: Maize is found most widely in the Americas, where it is a native species, and the United States is the world's largest producer. However, the crop is also grown extensively in Asia, China in particular, Europe, especially France, as well as Australia and parts of Africa, and for that matter, just about every other country around the globe.

the Anglo Saxon *fealo,* means pale red or pale yellow, the colour of ploughed but unsown land.) Other problems arose where the surrounding trees were felled for house fires and the scrub was grazed to death by sheep and goats. Without sheltering windbreaks, the precious topsoil was whipped away by the winter winds or washed down the watercourses by the rains.

There was (and still is) the problem of compaction, too. The nature of the small, intensively farmed open fields close to the village was changing. Crisscrossed by village traffic – the feet of planters and harvesters, the ox and the cart – the soil hardened, pooling the rain and cracking open in dry weather. Plants languished and died in such poorly drained soil.

If soil erosion, exhaustion and compaction plagued the new agriculturalists, it was nothing compared to the problems that would face farmers 8,000 years later. Today, with two agricultural revolutions already behind us (the first when farming began, the second when farming was mechanised in the 20th century) and a third, heralded by the genetic modification of crops and animals, underway, the same scenarios are being played out on a global scale. A study by the International Soil Reference and Information Centre estimated that an area the size of Canada and the United States combined – over 12 million square kilometres or 7.5 million square miles – had been lost to erosion and desertification, impacting on the lives of 250 million people worldwide. As historians continue trying to pinpoint the reason behind the founding of the world's first fields, scientists are struggling to see how the field is to survive into the future.

The New Kingdom

The future of the field in what might be called the New Kingdom – the Americas – has worried world organisations ever since Franklin D. Roosevelt declared, 'The history of every nation is eventually written in the way in which it cares for its soil.' The fields of the American continents, from Canada to Argentina, are vulnerable to erosion, exhaustion and compaction. Yet the fertility of these fields fed successive societies including the Maya and Aztecs, the Moche, Chimú and Inca civilisations of the Peruvian Andes, and the Hohokam, Mogollon and Anasazi civilisations.

The Moche farmed the land along the coast of northern Peru between around 100 and 800 C.E. Away from the lush river valleys, much of this land is now an inhospitable stretch of desert between one of the world's most fish-rich seas and the fertile slopes of the Andes, where llamas are raised and beans and potatoes grow. Two thousand years ago this was a green and productive plain with twice as much land under cultivation, thanks to the Moche, who were among the most accomplished of the early farmers. They employed a sophisticated system of water channels (the dried-out remains of which are still visible in the dirt today) to irrigate the plain. The Moche were succeeded by the Chimú and eventually the Inca nation, which defeated the Chimú in 1476 and went on to build the largest empire ever witnessed in the Andes. Within a century they had fallen prey to the Spanish conquistadores, the irrigation systems dried up, and the fields turned to dust.

The principal site of the agricultural revolution in pre-Columbian America, however, was centred around the hills and valleys of what is now Mexico. At Tehuacán, in central Mexico, the land is widely irrigated and intensively farmed. Around 5,000 years ago, fields were formed in these valleys when the Tehuacanos set up home and planted their grains, beans, squashes and chilies. But the wonder crop of prehistory – the 'gift of God' as the Maya called it – was first grown at about the same time in the Oaxaca Valley, around 200 kilometres (125 miles) south. This was maize, or corn. Protein-rich crops can build civilisations and corn proved to be the super-fuel of the Mayans, contributing to the founding of what was almost certainly the first major urban centre in the Americas, Monte Albán.

Another important high-energy food is manioc, the mealy flour extracted from the starchy root of bitter cassava, or the tapioca plant, which provides one of the highest yields of food energy per acre of any crop. The Maya were expert astronomers and mathematicians; they built cities dominated by great stone palaces and pyramids topped with temples where they celebrated the rebirth of the sun every dawn and kept peace with their gods through grisly human sacrifices. In fact, they owed a greater debt of gratitude to manioc. Rich in carbohydrates and low in protein, it is a vital secondary crop. (When Europeans took manioc from America to West Africa, the root and leaves, fermented in beer,

'The history of every nation is eventually written in the way in which it cares for its soil.'

Franklin D. Roosevelt, 1 March, 1936

were all used. But when it became the staple crop for subsistence farmers, the lack of protein led to severe malnutrition.)

In 1979, archaeologists unearthed the remarkable little village of Cerén, 15 miles west of El Salvador. These Maya villagers had just finished their day's work when the nearby volcano of Loma Caldera suddenly erupted, around 1,400 years ago. Like the Italian cities of Pompeii and Herculaneum, the village of Cerén was buried under choking volcanic ash up to 5 metres (17 feet) deep, perfectly preserving it in time. Uncovering the final, fatal moments of this farming community, archaeologists found no human remains under the debris. Had the villagers fled, warned by earth tremors? Instead, they unearthed an early August evening when the farm implements had been brought into the huts while the bedding had yet to be rolled out. And nearby were the manioc fields – long, parallel lines of planting beds up to 1.2 metres (4 feet) wide and separated by footpaths. On the afternoon of their last day, the villagers had been planting their manioc slips, or cuttings, into the earth, each slip armed with a couple of buds below ground to root the plant and one bud above to grow into the bush. Proof of the cultivation of this calorie-rich tuber has gone a long way towards explaining how the Maya succeeded in becoming one of the great civilisations of the Americas.

Europe's Oldest Fields

Over 4,000 years before the volcanic eruption at Cerén preserved its unique slice of history, the dry-stone walls of Ireland's first fields were being laid. And there they remained, undiscovered beneath the peat until the 1930s, when an amateur historian, musing over the rocks, looked more closely at their origins. In the absence of trees, peat and turf have traditionally provided fuel for the hearth over much of Ireland. Although turf was easier to collect and lighter to carry, it radiated less heat than peat and its cutting destroyed good grazing pasture. It was more sustainable to take the peat-cutting spade (the 'slane' or *sléan*) to the peat

The field systems of northern Peru were originally developed by the Moche civilisation between 100 and 800 c.e. With their sophisticated network of irrigation canals, they created lush, productive plains in what would otherwise have been a dry, barren landscape. These fields would later be farmed by people of the Chimú and Inca civilisations.

deposits or 'hags'. Here, the *sleadór* or peat cutter had to 'keep a straight face' on the bank he was cutting or else be ridiculed as a clod cutter. He also had to leave three uncut steps for Saint Colmcille, who was said to put a curse on any sleadór who failed to leave him a means of escape after he was trapped in a peat-cutter's bog hole. But when the cottagers of Ballycastle in north Mayo drew their peat from hags, they cursed the beds of rock they frequently found buried deep in the ground. It took a local schoolmaster, Patrick Caulfield from Belderrig, to find a plausible explanation for the bothersome stones. They presented a pair of mysteries: they lay under several thousand years of peat, and yet their arrangement suggested the work of human hands.

Peat is the mushy remains of swamp vegetation, laid down over a deep litter of pine left behind by ancient coniferous forests. Beneath these forests were the detritus of hazel, oak and elm, the hardwoods that colonised the land after the last ice age. The wet peat contains little of the oxygen that triggers the process of decay, and acts like a partial vacuum. As a result, Europe's peat bogs, especially those in Denmark and Ireland, regularly yield well-preserved remains: the gruesome figure of a young man ritually executed 2,000 years before; a Bronze Age cooking pit; a hoard of Celtic weapons; even the occasional tub of medieval butter, which in the 19th century fetched a good price as a high-quality grease for wagon axles. A cross-section through the peat reveals a deep slice of history, and the Ballycastle stones lay at the very bottom of the timeline, in the Neolithic era.

As Caulfield exposed more stones, or probed the peat with iron rods to trace their course, the invisible pattern of paths and boundaries began to uncover one of the oldest-known field systems in the world. The Céide fields (*Céide* means a flat-topped hill) were revealed as the remains of the field walls, homes and tombs of some of the earliest societies. The stones, which had been casually thrown aside by the peat cutters of Ballycastle, represented a gateway to Neolithic village life. (Country people often have a careless acquaintance with prehistoric remains. A visitor, admiring one of the many megaliths found in fields in western Ireland, was told by the farmer's red-haired daughter, 'Ah, they make a terrible nuisance. Father has had to dynamite some of the worst to clear a space.')

These Irish field forms (and others yet to be discovered) were the construct of the Neolithic people who preceded the great civilisations that lay on the historical horizon. The Neolithic era marks the stage when *Homo sapiens* replaced their chipped stone tools with ground or polished ones – in Greek, *neolithic* means 'new stone'. It was a vital forwards step in prehistory that occurred separately in different parts of the world at different times. In the 19th century, Eskimos and Australian Aborigines were still emerging from their own Stone Ages. But it was not the Neolithic people's gradual utilisation of stonework or pottery and metal that makes them so significant; it was their adoption of the field. And as they advanced through Europe, Asia and America, moving like a breeze across a savannah, their first fields signified the most radical transformation of the environment. Never mind roads or the Manhattan skyline – the field was going to change the face of the world.

The First Field Names

Every field has a name. One field may look like another to the country visitor, yet each possesses its own shape, peculiarities and character, and a farmer could name them all, just as he could every lane, path or road in the neighbourhood. Field names were part of the verbal map of the district. Some titles were simple geographical descriptions: High Field, Les Hauts Champs ('High Fields' in Switzerland), Creek Meadow, Le Champ au Chêne (the Oak Field), Campo Cresta (Ridge Field), Glebe (Church Land) or Bank Bottom. Some earned their title from a crop that grew well there: Flax Meadow, Champ de Blé (Wheat Field) or Hay Close. The name might celebrate a forgotten event or a topographical feature: Cae Tricornel (in Welsh, Three-Corner Field), Dancing Green, Les Forges (The Forge or Blacksmith's Field), May Field, Roman Camp, Church Pitch, or La Fontaine (Fountain or Spring Field). It might, and often did, refer to some long-dead owner: Pampas de Juanita, Raymond's Pitch, Murray's Meadow, Le Champ au Père Veyre. Field names can survive for centuries. The Scottish author Martin Martin revealed some mysterious field names when, in 1698, he published his account of the life of a group of remote islanders. Almost entirely illiterate, the islanders nevertheless appeared to have adopted the academic language of ancient Latin to describe certain fields on the island.

Today, Soay sheep, the relics of breeds farmed between 2,000 and 4,000 years ago, graze the wet pastures of the island moored in the North Sea above the British Isles. The sheep survive with no one to pluck the wool (Soay sheep were 'rooed' or plucked rather than sheared), for the island was abandoned after 1,200 years of occupation. In 1930, the families dragged their goods and chattels down

'Their arable land is very nicely parted into ten divisions ... each division distinguished by the name of some deceased man or woman, who were natives of this place.'

Martin Martin, *A Late Voyage to St. Kilda*, 1698

to the quay, drowned their sheep dogs in the harbour, and sailed forever from the land. This is St. Kilda, the lonely granite outcrop 64 kilometres (40 miles) west of the Outer Hebrides.

The salt-laden air of the windswept island made it difficult to wrest a crop from the fields. Nevertheless, the 200 or so islanders divided the hundred acres of farmable land up between each family. As Martin described in *A Late Voyage to St Kilda*: 'Their arable land is very nicely parted into ten divisions, and these into subdivisions, each division distinguished by the name of some deceased man or woman, who were natives of this place.' However, he added that 'there is one spot called *multa terra,* another *multa agris.*' Had Martin hit upon some original Latin names that had passed down from generation to generation since Roman times? The names *multa terra* and *multa agris* harked back to the days when the islands were first colonised by sixth- and seventh-century Christians, the monks who sailed from Ireland seeking solitude and bringing with them their second language: Latin. When St. Kilda was occupied, the 'parliament' (the men who met in the village's main, and only, street) reviewed the fielding arrangements every three years. Each group of fields was reallocated to a different family – a system known as *runrig* in the Scottish Highlands and Islands (the 'rig' was the ridge of land created by the plough). The system ensured that every family had the chance to benefit from the best, and suffer with the worst, of the land for a limited period.

The Céide fields on the northwest coast of Ireland are among the oldest field systems in the world. Discovered in the 1930s by a local schoolteacher named Patrick Caulfield, who recognised the scattered remains of their stone walls, these Neolithic fields pre-date both Stonehenge and the pyramids of ancient Egypt.

Rig and *multa terra* have survived for over a thousand years. Other field names can be found in land sale registers and marriage contracts where there was an exchange of land, and family historians occasionally trace an ancestral family to an old field title. Even while field names in the more industrialised parts of the world are being replaced by bland-but-efficient codes of letters and numbers, old field names live on in the phone book: Springfield, Oregon, Meadowbank, Auckland, Dordogne, Les Hauts Champs, Lausanne – the list goes on.

The Final Fields

For thousands of years, farmers have consciously selected the plants and animals that carried the traits they liked, and unconsciously the genes that caused them: the apple that kept well, the hop that fruited early, the goat with the more lustrous hide. And they would cross their best crop or animal with other top performers, hoping to hit upon a winning strain or encourage the development of certain desirable attributes. Whether planned or accidental, field history is founded on the successful outcome of such events. Richard Fuggle of Kent, England, discovered a hop growing in the village of Horsmonden in 1861 and took it home for cultivation. His resulting Fuggles hop went on to account for 90 per cent of the hops used to flavour and preserve British beer. However, cross-breeding was always a hit-and-miss affair and disappointing results inevitably outnumbered the successes.

All of this began to change in the 1950s, when scientists cracked the code of DNA and genetic modification gave the laboratory a serious role in the field. Each plant cell contains genes that determine how that plant will grow and harvest. Genetic modification, or GM, allows the scientist to track these genes and to transfer genes from one plant to another, even from one organism to another. Its detractors describe it as 'Frankenstein's foods'; while GM supporters counter with the claim that the GM fields could one day be the only way to feed a world in which the global population is increasing inexorably.

Work on GM crops began in the mid-20th century and the first GM plants were bred in the 1980s. The first successful commercial GM crop, tomatoes, was harvested in 1994. By 2005, GM crops were being grown in 21 countries around the world, mostly concentrated in the United States, Argentina, Brazil and Canada, where soya beans, maize, cotton, canola, squashes and papayas constitute the main crops.

However, not everyone is happy to accept this new marriage of science and agriculture. When GM seeds were tested in parts of England and Scotland in the late 1990s and early 2000s, for example, the experimental crops were attacked by angry protestors, who feared that GM crops would pollute the natural indigenous crops, and who accused the multinational corporations that developed the technology of seeking to dominate the world of seed supplies. And it isn't only in wealthy countries that opposition has appeared. Even in Mali, despite being the world's fourth poorest nation, farmers were resisting the march of GM cotton. GM can feed the world, claimed the GM lobby; GM only feeds the shareholders, countered its critics.

GM crop scientists argue that the new technology could produce an almost inconceivable range of benefits to society. They could be bred to clean land contaminated by explosives, create a harvestable replacement for plastics and detergents, and even kill the predatory caterpillars that threatened to eat them. A disease-resistant GM potato could fight back against blight; GM tobacco plants could be bred to produce a harvest of anti-HIV drugs in a process dubbed 'pharming'; GM hens could lay eggs containing vital proteins for use in the drugs war against cancer. As we approach the end of the first decade of the new millennium, some countries continue to resist the growing of GM crops, but ultimately the proliferation of GM may prove to be unstoppable. GM crops smuggled into countries yet to agree to grow them have already contaminated ordinary cereal crops. The European Union reports that up to a fifth of rice crossing its border is already contaminated with an illegal GM strain from the United States. While issues of global importance continue to arise and many important questions remain unanswered, one thing is certain: it looks as if the scene is already set for the fields of the future.

Chapter Two

SHAPING
THE LANDSCAPE

From the paddy fields of Asia to the pastures of New Zealand, and from the water meadows of northern Europe to the North American grain prairies, fields have had such influence upon the environment that they have come to symbolise the parts of the globe in which they are found. But how is it that fields have come to have such a defining role in shaping our landscapes?

The World of Fields

Viewed from above, the chequerboard of the world's fields is quite remarkable. And it must have been even more so to the world's first air travellers, Jean-François Pilâtre de Rozier and François Laurent d'Arlandes, aboard the Montgolfier brothers' hot-air balloon in 18th-century France. Joseph-Michel and Jacques-Étienne Montgolfier's innovation had first been unveiled in 1782, before further demonstrations – including tethered flights above Versailles – were made over the course of the following year. However, it was on 21 November, 1783, that what is widely acknowledged as the first free flight by humans was made. Of course, much has changed since Pilâtre de Rozier and his compatriot d'Arlandes drifted over Paris, but we have wondered at the aerial view of the world ever since.

In spite of the fact that air travel has since become relatively commonplace, the view of the world from above still excites the popular imagination. More recently, thanks to the proliferation of satellite imaging and the power of the Internet, it has become accessible to millions through the medium of Google Earth. This revelation has allowed millions of viewers the opportunity to soar high above the land and sea, and provides an arresting view of the world's fields from above.

From above, a viewer can gaze upon an array of forms and patterns: squares of tulips quartered by canals in Holland; or vast, neat rectangles of corn in neighbouring Germany; the perfectly circular green fields of Spain, traced by

The abstract pattern created by the circular fields of Gray County, Kansas, is broken only by the river running through them. The unusual shape is defined by their rotating irrigation systems.

the rotating booms of their irrigation systems; and the curious notch of woodland that marks the traditional pheasant cover of an English game-shooting field.

Paddy fields descend Asian hillsides like a verdant mantle of fish scales peppered with peasant huts, while in northern Italy they ascend Alpine valleys like the terraces of a giant's garden. In Cumbria, England, upland fields are stitched together by silvery limestone walls; while in France, south-facing Burgundian hillsides are strung with vines.

As well as providing texture and pattern, a field's crops also colour the view: the black of dried field beans; the chrome yellow of flowering oilseed rape; the pastel blue of a field of flax; the white stripes of ripening cotton; and the chain mail of semi-circular stone walls sheltering the vines of the Canary Isles.

Lavender, sunflowers, hops, olives, almond trees, vines, date palms – each crop adds a different texture and colour to the land, while the seasons rub along from spring greens and summer golds to the reds, greys and browns of autumn's ploughed fields. This aerial view of fields is as susceptible to the vagaries of the weather as the crops are below – obscured by mist, burned grey by drought, or submerged under snow, leaving lonely lines of fence posts to mark the fields' boundaries.

However, this view from above reveals more than just a pretty picture; indeed, such an overview can reveal sickness or health in the soil below: for example, brown paddy fields embossed with grassy bunds, compared with salt-encrusted rectangles, the infertile result of over-irrigation; or a peninsula patterned with emerald-green fields, each sheltering behind its own stone walls, juxtaposed with an estuary stained muddy brown by soil leaching from poorly protected fields.

Inspiring Fields

Of course, satellite imagery, no matter how detailed, cannot easily capture the play of sunlight and shade across the patchwork of fields. But such scenes have fascinated the artists of the world for many centuries, and they can render such nuances far more effectively. For the Japanese painter Katsushika Hokusai (1760–1849), the paddy fields and bunds beneath Mount Fuji were integral to his stylised view of the mountain itself. The radical French Impressionists Pierre-Auguste Renoir (1841–1919) and Edouard Manet (1832–83) both featured the field in their work as they painted *en plein air,* in the open air, as did the post-Impressionist Paul Cézanne (1839–1906). In fact, when one interviewer asked the most famous Impressionist of them all, Claude Monet (1840–1926), about his studio, the artist gestured at the landscape of northern France and declared: 'That is my studio.'

So intrigued was Monet by a group of haystacks in a Normandy field that he painted them again and again – as he would the lilies at his studio home in Giverny – in mist, in snow, at dawn, at dusk. When he exhibited the series *Haystacks* in 1891 the reviewers criticised his subject matter as banal and commonplace. Yet within days every painting was sold.

In the 20th century, the Dutch artist Piet Mondrian (1872–1944) embraced the neat, ordered landscape of his childhood haunts in his rectangular abstracts; while the Mexican surrealist Frida Kahlo (1907–54) often adopted agricultural scenes as backgrounds to her many self-portraits. When she was in a positive, reflective mood, she would portray the lush, rich vegetation of Mexico; when she was in emotional and physical pain it was the barren badlands that figured in her work.

The relatively recent art of photography has also made its contribution, and field portraits from the likes of Ansel Adams (1902–84) – although more famous for his work in U.S. national parks – have become a cornerstone of the medium. But when the French photographer Yann Arthus-Bertrand (b. 1946) took his

Haystacks in Giverny by Claude Monet, 1893. One of a number of studies that the great Impressionist made of this characteristic feature of the French landscape.

camera on a series of balloon flights over Kenya in the 1970s, it led to major change in the way fields are viewed. Arthus-Bertrand's ensuing collection of field and crop portraits found enormous popularity when published as *The Earth from the Air,* and subsequent exhibitions and new editions have proven its enduring appeal. Now the field has been revealed – whether in intimate aerial portraits or the spectacular panoramas of satellite images – not just as the subject of art, but as art itself. As Arthus-Bertrand himself says, 'The Earth is art.'

Paddy Fields

To grow one of the most important crops in the world, some 12 million square kilometres (4.6 million square miles) of land in Southeast Asia, America, Africa, Australasia and southern Europe – Italy especially – are devoted to the rice paddy field. A paddy (from the Malay for 'rice plant') is a field that has been flooded with water and where rice, sown and germinated in nurseries, is planted out after four weeks. Around 12 weeks later, depending on the climate, the rice, warmed by the soupy waters of the paddy, is ready to harvest.

Dry fields of rice can be raised – the rice grown like any other cereal – but it is the paddy field that accounts for more than 90 per cent of the 600 million metric tons of rice grown worldwide. The paddy field, spilling down a hillside or flowing like a green sea across a valley floor, remains the quintessential rice field.

Paddy fields must have a neighbouring stream, marsh or irrigation channel, and low mud banks, or bunds, are built to retain the water. In many places, paddy fields are stepped into the hillside in a series of tumbling terraces, dotted with small temples to the rice deities. The Balinese call such arrangements *subak* – a subak being a co-operative of rice growers who work fields with a shared water supply – and these are responsible for some of the archetypal landscapes of Indonesia.

It is most likely that the paddy originated in China – although the oldest known paddy fields are those of South Korea. On the terraced country hillsides of northern China wheat rather than rice is grown, but in the south it is the paddy field that dominates. Traditionally women have planted and weeded the crop while men have irrigated and ploughed the fields.

The ideal draft animal was, and still is, the water buffalo, a patient creature capable of drawing the plough and manuring the crop at the same time; however, it causes some surprising environmental problems. When rice roots, stalks and buffalo manure decay below the surface of the paddy field they produce a gas that bubbles to the surface as methane. High levels of methane have been identified as a significant cause of global warming and, despite managing their paddy fields in a sustainable, low-impact way, the rice farmers have found themselves unwittingly contributing to climate change. However, a simple solution is to empty the paddy between crops: draining the fields in this way reduces methane levels and also, by aerating the soil, increases the fertility of the paddies.

Irrigation

As exemplified by the paddies, water is the lifeblood of the field, and unless it rises in a field spring – some farmers find it more profitable to bottle and sell the spring water than farm the land – it must be brought to the field.

An eagle's-eye view of arid land reveals the occasional filigree of green where plants cling to the course of a stream, or rising with the water, keep it company until it peters out in the dirt. Oases like these always provided tribal people with the opportunity to found a field or two, to harvest a cash crop of figs or dates, or a stand of barley. Eventually, following nature's example, farmers started to irrigate the land themselves, and they have done so ever since.

At nightfall in the Hindu Kush, Afghan farmers still lift the little shutters on the irrigation canals to let the water onto the land, just as they have done for at least 2,000 years. Watering the land was central to field makers as far and wide as Mesopotamia, China – major irrigation works supported the Qin dynasty from around 221 to 206 B.C.E. – and the Andes. In the classical world, the Roman Empire, which once reached from the Atlantic Ocean to the Black Sea, not only supplied much of the land with water directed along stone aqueducts – three of which still function today in Rome itself – but also gave us the word 'irrigate' (from *irrigare*, meaning 'to moisten'). Then, through the Middle Ages, irrigation schemes on the part of Europe's monasteries brought vast swathes of land under cultivation, while Muslim engineers supplied thousands of Iberian farmers with the tiled *alberca,* or reservoir, and village squares with their drinking troughs and spring-fed pools, or *balsas.*

This brief history reflects the perennial problem of distributing water equitably. Irrigation brings new life to dry lands, but inevitably leads to problems such as overgrazing and thin soils being lost to erosion. On arid land, water used for irrigation will evaporate quickly, sucking mineral salts up to the surface – a

RICE

Name: Rice
(*Oryza sativa*)

What it's like: Depending on the variety – of which there are over 140,000 – rice grows to about 1 metre (3 feet) with the grain forming on a panicle of spikelets at the head of the stalk. In developing countries it is grown and harvested by hand. The fact that half the world's people depend on it makes rice the most important crop on the planet.

A member of the grass family, rice can be grouped into upland rice (grown on hillsides), rain-fed rice (in shallow water), irrigated rice (in paddy fields), and deep-water rice (in estuaries and places that flood naturally). Rice takes between 90 and 260 days to grow and it seeds about 30 days after flowering.

In the 19th century the switch from brown rice, which contains vitamins and proteins, to white or polished rice where the bran was removed, resulted in the increased incidence of beriberi, a disease caused by the lack of vitamin B_1. Synthetic vitamins are sometimes added to polished rice to compensate for the loss. Since the 1960s new varieties have seen rice yields double.

Where it's grown: Over a hundred countries grow rice, with more than 50 producing at least 100,000 metric tons a year. Asian farmers produce about 90 per cent of the world's rice, and the paddy fields of China and India grow more than half the world's total crop of 645 million metric tons. Latin America grows around 75 per cent of the upland rice, and huge areas of rainforest have been cleared in order to accommodate the crop.

process known as salination – and gradually poisoning the soil. In extreme circumstances the land can become infertile and the people who farm there will be forced to abandon it.

There has been no lasting rolling-back of the world's deserts, although nations continue to try. One example from the pages of history is the city of Urkesh, which flourished in the late third millennium B.C.E. in what is now Syria. This city was once one of the most significant in the Fertile Crescent, but today the sun beats down on bare rock and the crumbled stone of abandoned houses – the result of over-irrigation. Today, Saudi Arabia irrigates its crops with rainwater stored in aquifers deep underground, and has become an exporter of wheat. But the rainwater that irrigates today's corn fell up to 30,000 years ago. It may well be gone in a century. Already, according to UNESCO, some 10 per cent of the world's irrigated land has been lost to desert.

Polders and Fens

At the other extreme from the irrigation of otherwise arid lands is the *polder* – a Dutch word for the dry bed of a lake – which is an area of land reclaimed from the waters by using walls, drains, dikes and pumps. Such reclamation can be found around the world, but most famously in the Netherlands, where more than a quarter of the land requires protection from the sea.

There is a famous story of a young boy who was making his way home at dusk near the Dutch town of Haarlem when he spotted a leak in a dike. Left overnight, the leak would grow and by morning be delivering a torrent of water onto the fields, drowning stock and flooding homes. The plucky youngster climbed the bank of the dike, plugged the leak with his own hand, and remained there through the night until help arrived.

Although a statue commemorates the event, there was no such boy. The tale was the creation of American author Mary Elizabeth Mapes Dodge in her 1865 story *The Silver Skates*. Her tale does, however, underline the inherent dangers of life on the polder, living close to, or even below, sea level.

Across the North Sea from the Netherlands, there can be found similar low and marshy fields, surrounded by water, in England's East Anglian Fens. Here some 240 kilometres (150 miles) of navigable rivers wind their way between grazing meadows, pools and lagoons, which provided one young seaman, Horatio Nelson, the hero of Trafalgar, with a place where he could learn to sail.

The Fens were created when the pits and channels of medieval peat diggers flooded suddenly in the 14th century, and by the 17th century the Fenland farmers wanted more from their fields. Down the centuries, they had traded everything from sheep, beer and house tiles with their Dutch neighbours across the sea, and in 1640 they turned to a new import – hydro-technology. A Netherlander, Cornelius Vermuyden, who had been helping English farmers learn how the Zeeland farmers grew the dyers' plant madder (*Rubia tinctoria*), was making a name for himself as a drainage engineer. Now he was brought in to devise new drainage systems, based on those from Roman times, for the Fens. His reclamation work produced some of the richest fields in Britain.

The Dutch were the acknowledged masters of land reclamation – one engineer being known as Jan Leeghwater, literally 'empty water'. Their success was partly due to pressing a familiar agricultural machine into service: the mill. Powered either by water or wind, mills were designed to grind maize. But from the hydro-engineer's point of view they could be linked to a pump instead of millstones.

Windmills came in two basic forms: post mills and tower mills. The post mill was built with the sails and machinery constructed inside a cabin-like superstructure, mounted on a sturdy, central, timber post. The whole cabin could be revolved on the post, turned by hand or horse, so that the sails were set to meet the prevailing wind. The tower mill was a more permanent structure. The grinding or pumping equipment was housed inside the brick tower while the sails were set on a revolving cap constructed on top of the tower. A fan tail, mounted on the rotating cap, acted like the fin of a weather vane, turning the sails into the wind.

'Quick as a flash, he saw his duty.
Throwing away his flowers, the boy clambered
up the heights until he reached the hole.
His chubby little finger was thrust in,
almost before he knew it.
The flowing was stopped!'

Mary Elizabeth Mapes Dodge, *Hans Brinker or the Silver Skates*, 1865

The first recorded water-pumping windmill was in 14th-century Belgium, and the first in Holland in 1408. Built by the thousands along the canal banks, Holland's post and tower mills kept the sea from the land. At the height of the Industrial Revolution, over 40 per cent of the drainage was powered by the revolving sails of the windmill, and only when cheap coal became available to power steam engines did the windmills fall into decline. By then, however, the mill had come to be irrevocably linked with the Dutch landscape, not least in the works of artists such as Mondrian (see page 37).

Drowners and Water Meadows

To the casual onlooker a water meadow is a pretty field close to the river, blessed with buttercups and grazed by fat, contented cattle. To the farmer, however, it is a carefully engineered environment and a ready source of cash.

Water meadows should not be confused with flood meadows, which are naturally covered by seasonal flooding from a river. Regularly inundated each winter, water meadows reappeared in spring enriched with a fresh layer of riverine silt. Less susceptible to late frosts, they also produced good pastures at the start of the grazing season. Agriculturalists used some simple engineering to artificially flood and drain the water meadow and thus increase its efficiency. They dug sloping ditches to carry the water to the upriver pasture, and drain it at the downriver end, and constructed a system of ridges and furrows, which sloped parallel with the river's flow, to help spread the water across the field. Irrigation brought the grass-growing season forwards by several weeks and also kept the grass growing in dry weather.

Employed from the early days in Switzerland's Zermatt Valley and elsewhere in the Italian Alps and Britain, the art of water-meadowing lay in bringing just enough water onto the pasture as early in the year as possible, and draining it from the land as quickly as possible before the sheep or cattle were let loose on the spring grazing. To use the analogy of a horse, the idea was to make the water enter the field at a trot and leave at a gallop.

The craft of managing the water meadow fell to the 'drowner' or waterman, and the more level the meadow the greater his skills needed to be. The drowner would use his tracing 'knife', a J-shaped blade, to cut and re-edge his mains (the channels that carried the water onto the meadow) and drains (the channels that drew the water off and back to the river again).

One element that improved the water meadow's fertility was what one 16th-century English commentator described as 'euery mannes mydding', or everyone's dunghill up river. If the waterman was a skilful exponent of the craft of drowning, he could claim to be able to quadruple the fertility of the fields.

Once the meadow had been 'floated', the early grass began to grow, and sheep, which were about to lamb or had just lambed, would be pastured on the new grass. In late spring the sheep were moved to new grass elsewhere, and the water meadow was allowed to grow until the swish of the sickle signalled the start of the hay harvest. The grass would be mown, dried, stacked and ricked close to the farm, in store for the winter. Then it was the turn of the young cattle to come and feed, and with their manure to fertilise the meadow until the flooding cycle started again. However, there was one inherent disadvantage: sometimes the river would flood without warning, drowning the poor creatures trapped on the field and sometimes even the unlucky farmhand sent to their rescue.

Plantations and Pests

The contrast between the meandering water meadow and the symmetry of a plantation is striking. Palm oil, bananas, tea, sugar cane, cacao, coffee, cotton, sugar, sisal, pineapples, nuts, even cider apples: all have been grown on a great scale in the regimented fields of the plantation. Large plantations still occupy some of the best land in Malaysia, Peru, India and Africa. Plantations were often the work of colonisers who turned virgin territory, or more often native lands, into fields of exportable products through the use of cheap labour.

Although the plantations provided a regular income for local labourers – unless they were worked by slaves – and an exportable cash crop, they were also vulnerable to the boom-and-bust cycle of international trade. In the early 20th century, plantations devoted to the rubber trade had the potential to generate huge profits. Rubber had begun to be exported from the interior of East Africa – the exports proved more profitable than the slave trade – in the late 19th century. Later, large rubber plantations were planted by British colonists in Malaysia and by the Dutch in Indonesia, replacing the native forests.

Early water-meadow patterns in the Zermatt Valley, Switzerland, reveal drainage systems that increased the efficiency of the old water meadow.

In a particularly underhand episode, the seeds required for these plantations – from the Brazilian rubber tree (*Hevea brasiliensis*) – had been stolen from Brazil. The Brazilians had tried to preserve their growing assets, but were persuaded to gift some seeds to Queen Victoria. Instead they were sent to the Royal Botanic Gardens, Kew, London, in 1876, and while a virulent attack of South American leaf blight doomed the native rubber trade in the Americas, Kew's seeds were sown and raised and sent instead to Malaysia, where they would form the backbone of the eastern rubber trade.

In the plantations of India, Thailand and Indonesia, the trees were tapped for their sticky latex, which was taken from just beneath the bark, and processed into the rubber utilised for everything from tires to contraceptives. The development of the petrochemical and plastics industry during, and after, the Second World War, and the Japanese occupation of the rubber plantations at that time were setbacks for the rubber growers; but the synthetic varieties were no match for the natural product; indeed, aircraft wheels still rely on real rubber.

Since colonial times, plantation owners have generally been the wealthiest landlords in the region and even radical land reforms have been insufficient to cede the best fields back into local hands. In Ecuador, where farming supports half the population, land reforms were introduced in the late 20th century to try to resolve land distribution problems stemming from as far back as the Spanish conquest. The farms, or *sierra haciendas*, extended from valley floor to mountain crest, but while the fertile valleys were farmed by the plantation owners, the peons were left with the marginal, steeper land. Even after reforms, the small farmers were left working the subsistence lands of the upper plateau, while the coastal plantation owners continued to grow their sugar cane, cacao and bananas for export on the lower, more fertile coast and valleys.

The orderly pattern of the plantation masks another problem. Growing the same crop season after season in the same place makes it susceptible to pests and disease. For instance, in the Périgord region of France in the 1860s a quarter of the cultivated land was under the wine makers' vines. At the time some 90 per cent of the people worked the land when, in 1868, the pest phylloxera struck the crops. Introduced from North America sometime in the previous decade, these tiny, sap-sucking insects, related to aphids, fed on the roots of the grapevines. The ancient vineyard fields simply failed one by one in the Great French Wine Blight. Some farmers were rescued by a new plant crop, tobacco – it led the region to become France's second-largest grower – but the countryside was so devastated that, a century later, vineyards still stood empty and forlorn.

O A T

Name: Oat
(*Avena sativa*)

What it's like: Oats grow in the same way as the other cereal crops, wheat, barley and rye. An erect stalk around waist high branches out and the grain, or oats, hang in spikelets from the ends of the branches.

Oats can grow at higher altitudes than either wheat or barley. They are a high-energy food and can be cut green, or unripened, or harvested and threshed before being turned into foods such as oatcakes or porridge. In his 1755 *Dictionary of the English Language*, the

scholar Dr. Samuel Johnson wrote that the oat was a grain 'generally given to horses, but in Scotland supports the people.' Oat porridge and oatcakes remain national favourites in that country, and remain the nearest modern food that we have to the cereal gruels that once formed the staple diet of Europe's peasants.

If oats are the farmer's friend, the wild oat (*Avena fatua*) certainly is not. When it appears in the cereal field it must be either sprayed or rogued – that is, pulled by hand and burned.

Where it's grown: Oats like a cool, moist climate and grow in Europe and North America, with Canada, the United States, Russia, Finland and Poland the leading oat producers. In Scotland the oat plays a significant role in the cropping systems.

All too often, monocropping creates a vulnerability to pests and disease that leaves only one solution: to pile on the agrochemical controls. As a consequence, non-organic cotton-field plantations have earned the dubious award of being the most intensively sprayed crop in the world.

Enclosures and Allotments

The fields of the world are scarred by history. Circular Bronze Age burial mounds pockmark a *clos* in Finistère, in northwest France. An Iron Age fort leaves a faint impression on a Danish hill top. The mounded remains of First World War trenchworks snake across a Belgian meadow. However, perhaps the most telling in the field's own history are the corrugations left behind by 1,200 years of open-field farming in the English Midlands. They are the vestiges of ridge-and-furrow farming, a system that came to an abrupt and controversial end during a period known as the Enclosures.

Enclosure is a process that is carried on across the world whenever land is brought into private or public ownership. The Great Plains of the American West were enclosed by barbed-wire fences to keep the cattle safe; great tracts of bush in southeastern Africa were enclosed to control the spread of foot-and-mouth disease. But England's enclosures, which resulted in one of the world's most distinctive landscapes of hedged fields, were shockingly quick and changed the face of the field forever.

Enclosure is the simple act of fencing a field, but to the 19th-century English peasant poet John Clare it was a penance on the poor: 'Inclosure, thou'rt a curse upon the land, And tasteless was the wretch who thy existence plann'd.' The wretch or wretches who planned the enclosures were the landowning gentry of England. Between about 1760 and 1820, the eve of the nation's Industrial Revolution, they parcelled up an estimated seven million acres of England.

In 1800 a journeyman tailor carrying his bolts of cloth to sell in the Leicestershire market town where he had been raised 40 years before would have been struck by the changes. In his childhood, great open fields up to 40 hectares (100 acres) and edged with woodland, meres and lakes had dominated the scene. The ground would have been rippled with plough marks, scored by muddy cart tracks and the grassy headlands where the plough was turned at the end of each strip of open field, and crisscrossed by meandering paths. Now the tailor would have looked across a rolling patchwork of squared-off fields edged with infant hedges of hawthorn and intersected by straight, wide coach roads. Even the meres had gone, for in the lust to put land to the plough, forest, moor and marsh had been felled, drained and enclosed.

Concentrated on the richer farmlands that lay along the broad strip between the southwestern shire of Dorset and the northeastern shire of Yorkshire, enclosures represented a radical change from subsistence farming to farming for gain. Although enclosures had been made beforehand, the process had begun in earnest with Henry VIII's Dissolution of the Monasteries from 1536 to 1541. In dissolving the great landowning monasteries, Henry closed them down and confiscated their land, gifting or selling it to his subjects. Initially the efforts of the new landowners to enclose were thwarted by churchmen and other landed gentry, but there was no stopping the pressure for agricultural change. And, over the course of the following century, when landowners who had been exiled during the English Civil War returned to their fields, they were imbued with new ideas such as four-crop rotation and new machinery such as Jethro Tull's seed drill. Armed with such innovations, they forced a series of enclosures across the English shires, each written into law in the form of an 'Inclosure Act'.

The enclosure movement peaked in the late 1700s and by the 1830s the medieval peasant community was at an end. To men like John Clare, enclosures represented the theft of the land from working families, and the end of sustainable and communal land use. The social consequences certainly prompted one agricultural board to note with concern that 'the poor are injured, in some, grossly injured.' But to the improvers, the enclosures heralded a more productive era and represented the best way to feed a burgeoning population. The argument over who was right still rumbles on.

One effect of the enclosures was the creation of the 'pauper's patch', or allotment: fields divided into small plots, almost like miniatures of the old open fields, where the commoners grew fruit and vegetables. The English allotment, from the Old French *aloter* meaning 'to divide and share', was one way to compensate for Clare's 'curse on the poor', and the first field of wasteland was 'allotted' in Wiltshire

'Inclosure, thou'rt a curse upon the land, And tasteless was the wretch who thy existence plann'd.'

John Clare, *The Village Minstrel*, 1821

in 1806. It was not without opposition, however, as landowners worried that their labourers might steal their seeds or conserve their energies during the day, and selfishly expend them on their own allotments in the evening. As one Victorian commentator warned: 'The extent of the garden of a labourer ought never to be such as to interfere with his employment as a labourer.'

In Europe and America the business of growing vegetables in smallholdings is more recent, dating back to the expansion of the cities in the late 1800s and early 1900s. As gardens were crowded out by factories and tenements, smallholders were forced to find land elsewhere. In France the poor had to make do with the *lopin de terre*, a vegetable plot squeezed into an urban corner. The more fortunate found space on *les jardins ouvriers*, grouped together like British allotments on the outskirts of a town. The German equivalent was the *Kleingarten*, a field or two where rows of vegetables and flowers grew beside the barbecue, the summerhouse and the social club. It was a model for the garden colonies that still stretch across Europe from Prague to Helsingborg today.

Open Fields

The pre-enclosure system of farming the arable fields close to the village in strips of land, and keeping herds of sheep, goats or cattle to graze the common pastures and woodland beyond, is an age-old agricultural model. It was practised the world over; and in remote areas it continues still.

The system relies on three main arable areas: one for winter grains such as wheat, barley or oats; one for spring grains; and one to lie fallow, resting for the year. There are other crops too: beans, peas and vetch for animal fodder; flax and hemp for making linen and canvas; and perhaps woad or teasels for the village cloth maker. In addition to the grazing common there would be a good hay meadow where the grass would be cropped and stored in ricks to feed animals through the winter, the remainder being slaughtered and their meat preserved.

The system had advantages and disadvantages. Open fields promoted social cohesion. As with the St. Kilda parliament (see page 29), the community had to work together; but there were also problems. For example, the villager who

The distinctive corrugations of a ridge-and-furrow field reveal a system that dated back over a thousand years, but was brought to an abrupt halt during the late 1700s.

found a good milking goat could neither improve the animal's bloodline nor protect it from endemic animal diseases if all the animals were grazed together.

Bit by bit common fields slipped into private ownership. Fencing fields involved owning the land – or at least laying claim to it in the knowledge that you could defeat anyone who dared dispute your claim. Enclosing land deprived some families of their livelihood, turning them into landless labourers who were gradually forced elsewhere, or reduced to squatting on the marginal, common land that was left. Squatters in northern Europe were considered to be at the very bottom of the social hierarchy.

In Australia the story was different: once a hiker could walk through the rainforests of eastern Australia and never encounter a gate. But by the mid-19th century the country was being parcelled up and sold to new settlers. There was no call for open fields here. 'Fencing and enclosing land is the greatest and most important improvement that can be effected upon it,' declared James Atkinson in his *Account of Agriculture and Grazing in New South Wales*, adding: 'It is the foundation and basis of every other improvement to be afterwards expected.'

Squatters simply moved outside official settlement limits to found their farms on wastelands. One frustrated governor, Sir George Gipps, described the effort of trying to restrict these 'graziers and woolgatherers' as trying to confine 'the Arabs of the Desert'. Some of Australia's squatters came from the ranks of the European poor, landless labourers whose forebears had been disinherited during the enclosures, and who now sought a new life down under. In time these squatters' land claims were legitimised and a new 'squattocracy' was born.

'Fencing and enclosing land is the greatest and most important improvement that can be effected upon it.'

James Atkinson, *An Account of Agriculture and Grazing in New South Wales*, 1826

Hedges

Look up on a clear night with a full moon, and trace the figure of the man in the moon. He is the dim-witted hedge mender carrying on his back a fork-load of thorns. He is away to repair a hedge, so they say.

According to Samuel Johnson the hedge denoted something 'mean, vile, of the lowest class' as with 'plying one's trade under a hedge', as with the hedge wench, or the hedge priest. But Caesar, before him, was much impressed by such obstacles, when pushing through northern Europe during the Gallic Wars: 'These hedges present a barrier like a wall', he wrote wonderingly.

The living hedge, protected by a ditch to keep browsing cattle at bay, was made by planting saplings of thorn, oak, crab, hawthorn and holly against a temporary stake-and-pole fence. Within a decade the saplings were tall enough to be 'laid' when the sap was down during the winter. The hedger would cut into the lower part of a sapling, bend it over, and weave it around fresh stakes cut from surplus timber. The top of the hedge was finished with a rail of willow or hazel – a willow bed often being planted nearby to provide the material.

One Thomas Tusser pointed out in his *Five Hundred Pointes of Good Husbandrie* in 1573: '… euerie [every] hedge hath plenty of fewell and fruit.' But anyone caught stealing that 'fewell', or fuel, faced being whipped until they 'bled well' for the offence of hedge breaking. And they would have to compensate the landowner who had to call on the man in the moon, the hedge mender, to make good the damage.

A dead hedge was an acceptable alternative to the living hedge. Indeed it was the original hedge of England, used to demarcate the process of *assarting*, the clearing of small areas of wasteland or woodland for farming. In Estonia, tall hazel rods (which the 16th-century English farmers called *ethers*) were woven between three horizontal poles; in Sweden, pine poles held together with a twist of bark rested at 45 degrees in a timber framework; in the timber-rich areas of Canada, pioneer farmers brought the old ways with them from Europe and marked out their fields with zigzag split-rail fences.

The purpose of the hedge ranged from delineating a commune's boundaries to enclosing a field, from partitioning off parts of an estate without resorting to the costly business of building in brick or stone, to keeping the farm animals in and predatory wolves and bears out. It became the dominant feature of the English landscape, later to be exported around the world to New England, New Zealand and even Tasmania by colonists.

Whether it is the Brazilian rainforest or the lakeside scrub of a pool in the Tatra Mountains, the older the habitat, the greater the number of plants and animals in it. The same holds true of hedges, which can be roughly dated by the number of species they harbour – although the margin of error is high.

To date a hedge, take ten paces along it counting the different species of plants as you go – it is best to avoid the hedge ends, especially where they join a woodland where other species may colonise them. Discount woody climbers such as honeysuckle, traveller's joy (*Clematis vitalba*) and ivy, and count different species of hedge rose as a single plant. Do this three or four times at different points to provide an average. Then multiply the number of species by 110 and add 30 years to the total. This would, for example, make a two-species hedge around a quarter of a millennium old, while a hedge with five species could date back over half a millennium; a six-species hedge could well have been planted when Europe was being ravaged by the second outbreak of the Black Death.

One of the strangest hedges in Europe – and also one with a suitably ancient history – is the Penny Hedge, built every year at the sea's edge in Whitby, England. This is the story of how it came about:

In 1159 three knights out hunting chanced upon and wounded a boar. The animal made a run for it. 'Hoy, hoy, hoy', cried the young blades as they drove their hounds in pursuit, out over the wild lands of Eskdale in northeast England. But the hog swerved away down a bank, bursting through the hedge of a hermitage. The men followed, driving their horses into the monastic close where a lone friar hoeing his field, and no friend of the hunters, put himself between the panting boar and the huntsmen. The hounds, crazed with the chase, turned on the unfortunate monk, savaging him before the men could reach him. They jumped from their horses and pulled back the hounds, but it was too late. The monk, mortally wounded, lay dying. In an act of benediction the old man forgave the hunters and breathed his last.

The Abbot of Whitby, where the monk lived, was less forgiving. He spared their lives on the condition that they built a penance hedge every year on the sea shore. 'Each of you shall set your Stakes at the Brim of the Water each Stake a Yard from another and so Yedder them, as with Yedders, and so stake on each side with your stout Stowers that they stand three tides without removing by the Force of the Water. You shall do this in remembrance that you did cruelly slay me.' If they failed in their task then their lands would be forfeited to the Abbot.

Every year the penance or Penny Hedge is still built on the Eve of Ascension Day (celebrated 40 days after Easter Sunday) in the wet sand of Whitby.

WILD OR DOG ROSE

Name: Wild or Dog Rose
(*Rosa canina*)

What it's like: Growing up to 5 metres (16 feet), the deciduous shrub has green, erect or arching stems each armed with stout, hooked thorns that were particularly good at keeping animals at bay when the rose was grown as a hedge plant. The Swedes called it their stone rose, the Danes, their thunder rose. The 17th-century English botanist Nicholas Culpeper described it thus: 'Called also wild rose, the dog-rose has winged leaves like garden roses, but smoother and greener; the flowers are single, of five white, and sometimes pale red leaves.' The flowers are followed by hips, 'roundish red seed-vessels, full of pulp, enclosing white cornered seed, covered with short stiff hairs.'

Dried and ground, the hairy seed has armed generations of recalcitrant schoolchildren with an efficient itching powder. While the hips had other useful ingredients, as Culpeper noted: 'The pulp has a pleasant, grateful acidity, strengthens the stomach, cools the heat of fevers, is pectoral, good for coughs and spitting of blood, and the scurvy.'

The hips were harvested during the Second World War to provide vital vitamin C to populations struggling to obtain adequate nutrition. (British schoolchildren collected 450 metric tons in one year.) And one cup of rosehip syrup offered as much vitamin C as 40 fresh oranges.

The flowers are softly scented. However, a more highly scented hybrid, later named Abbotswood, was discovered in the garden of the farm tractor magnate Harry Ferguson.

Where it's grown: Native throughout Europe, northwest Africa and western Asia, it has spread to other temperate areas.

'Such an innovation would brand the builder of walls for ever as a rebel against accepted convention, and damn him without redemption in the eyes of those prudent and sagacious persons who assess a man's reputation in Franche-Comté.'

Stendhal, *Le Rouge et le Noir,* 1830

Walls and Fences

Good fences make good neighbours, or so the saying goes. They also make safe fields; so the need to fence fields has exercised the farmer for centuries. Sunken fences, walls and wide watercourses have all played their part alongside the stock-proof hedge.

Water has proven an effective way to keep predators out and the farm animals in. One way of containing the rabbit warren in medieval times was to surround the field with a water-filled ditch.

Stone, on the other hand, was both a burden and a blessing for the farmer. On rocky terrain it was child's work, literally, to clear stones from the fields and pile them into field walls. Some of Europe's oldest stone walls still stand at Skara Brae on Orkney, Scotland, built between 3200 and 2200 B.C.E. (Skara Brae only came to light when a storm in 1850 stripped the grass from a local mound, exposing the Neolithic walls.) Most stone walls are infants by comparison. The geological seams of limestone that course through Europe make a pronounced appearance in the French Dordogne and the English Cotswolds. Most of these silvery stone boundaries date back to the monastic wool trade of the 13th and 14th centuries. For the poet William Wordsworth walls such as these could be said rather to have 'grown than to have been erected – to have risen by an instinct of their own, out of the native rock ... such is their wildness and beauty.' (His

Stone walls in Cumbria, England, now form an intrinsic part of the landscape, but the sheep walls were once condemned by the English Romantic poet William Wordsworth.

fondness for the look of these landscapes did not prevent him grumbling about the sheep farmers who 'scarred' his beloved Cumbrian fells with the stone walls that have become a widely admired part of the landscape two centuries later.) Many stone walls were built dry, that is without any binding mortar, and the stone waller's craft varied not just from country to country, but from village to village. While one group of wallers swore by their combers, the line of semi-circular coping stones used to finish off the top of the walls, another group would maintain that nothing could improve upon the crenellated, or 'cock and hen', finish.

The French writer Stendhal, also known as Henri-Marie Beyle (1783–1842), gave a clue to this rural conservatism in *Le Rouge et le Noir*: 'To win public esteem in Verrières, it is essential, while building walls, not to adopt any sort of plan imported from Italy by the stone masons passing every spring through the Jura gorges on their way to Paris. Such an innovation would brand the builder of walls for ever as a rebel against accepted convention, and damn him without redemption in the eyes of those prudent and sagacious persons who assess a man's reputation in Franche-Comté.'

Where there was too little stone, or it was unsuitable for dry stone walling, farmers demonstrated their customary resourcefulness by using stone to fortify earth banks, burying the stone beneath a soil mound or, in the old Celtic provinces of west Brittany, France, and Cornwall, England, laying the earth over a herringbone pattern of stone. In Ireland earth banks served as field boundaries. Where there was no stone, the earth itself was pressed into service. Across the world clay, pisé, clunch, clom and adobe were used to wall in the flock and keep out the wilderness. Such walls, sometimes protected from the rain by miniature roofs of clay tiles or thatch, also served as something of a status symbol. Reserved for use on the infields, the vegetable yard or paddock, they reminded the farmer's neighbours that here was a family of presence and prestige.

Away from the house field, walls gave way to fences made from whatever lay close to hand: cut-down thorn bushes, corrugated iron, even fangs of quarry slate waste stood on end and wired together to form a picket or paling fence (from the Latin *palus* or 'stake'). The primary purpose of the pale in the Middle Ages was not to keep out wild animals, but to keep fallow deer in the nobleman's hunting park. The medieval pale was made of split or cleft oak stakes set in the ground and nailed to horizontal rails. To make doubly sure the deer stayed in, a bank and ditch were added, the pale fence being run along the top of the bank.

In 1171 the conquest of Ireland by Henry II brought English settlers who lived within an area separated from the Irish, a region known as The Pale. Those living 'beyond the pale' were considered beyond redemption. In the 20th century the pale moved from fields to housing developments – the bright white picket fence so cherished by the suburban householder has curious antecedents.

The Devil's Rope

Barbed wire was, according to the Buenos Aires-born farmer's son and writer William Henry Hudson (1841–1922), 'man's improvement on the bramble'. But its use has not found universal favour, and according to the Native Americans who saw the Great Plains carved up by strands of wire, it was the Devil's rope; while for those caught on the battlefields of the First World War, it was known as gooseberry wire, for the fruiting bush's frightening array of thorns.

To underscore its importance, 'improved stock wire' was patented no less than nine times in the United States between 1868 and 1874, Michael Kelly registering the first 'thorny fence' with a double strand of wire fixed with barbs. Then an Illinois farmer, Joseph Glidden, patented his improved designs together with a machine for the manufacture of his brand known as 'The Winner'.

However, although such an effective material has found favour with farmers the world over, the irresponsible use of barbed wire is increasingly controversial. Indeed, such use has specifically been condemned by the legislature of Norway, where local authorities are also entitled to prohibit the use of barbed wire for fencing altogether, should they see fit.

This most controversial of the field's boundary markers serves to highlight the connection between the fields and the societies that tend them. Whether viewed from the ground or the air, fields' textures and forms, their patterns and boundaries are reminders of the many ways in which fields have shaped both the course of human history and the landscape in which we live.

Chapter Three

❦

BRAVE
NEW WORLDS

As humanity spread across the globe, so populations took their methods of farming with them. This led to the creation of some of the world's most productive fields and some of history's most tragic mistakes. Fields can make history. They can be the cause of radical social change. And the fields in this chapter are examples of this crucial influence.

Fields of Fleece

Some fields have a devastating impact on the people who work them, and the cotton field is one such example. Long before sail power bridged the gap between the Americas and Europe, cotton was used and grown around the world – wild cotton grew in the Sudan on the Upper Nile, Peru, Pakistan, Australia, anywhere with plenty of sunshine (a minimum of 160 days a year) and no risk of frost.

If people living in the Northern Hemisphere used sheep's wool for their work wear, the rest of the world relied on cotton, or what the bemused fifth-century B.C.E. historian Herodotus described as that wild plant 'that bears fleece exceeding in goodness and beauty that of sheep.'

The cotton field started to impact on local landscapes after being brought to Europe from India by Alexander the Great around 300 B.C.E., yet cotton remained a luxury item until Europe's fashionable ladies developed a taste for dreamy, cotton *indienne* gowns, and the working man for his denims – originally made from the cotton worked out of Nîmes (*serge de Nîmes*), in France.

Bales of the white stuff were imported from countries such as India, Surinam and Guyana to Britain, the major cotton-processing country – cotton came to represent 75 per cent of the raw materials that powered the British Industrial Revolution and it would underpin the founding of the London Stock Exchange. But as the demand grew and as the cotton processors invented ever more efficient machinery, cotton fields started to appear in Jamestown, Virginia, Barbados and Exuma in the Bahamas.

A North American cotton field was once where the wealth generated by the cotton crop was dependent on the miseries of the slave trade.

Instead of simply shipping it to Britain, America began to process cotton from its southern states. Before long it had become central to the economy: 'Cotton is king', declared the South Carolina senator James Henry Hammond, in 1858. As the banks started lending money to buy extra land, and that other requisite of the cotton trade, black slaves, the number of cotton fields grew. 900,000 metric tons (two billion pounds) of cotton were produced in 1855, when just 50 years earlier the fields had managed a mere 104 million pounds. As a result the slave population rose to 3.2 million – nearly half the total population of the southern states – with over half of the slaves working the cotton fields, often in appalling conditions. Children started in the cotton fields at the age of seven; their parents meanwhile were managed in gangs, at the tip of a bullwhip.

Cotton was sometimes grown with maize (corn), the two crops providing year-round work for the slaves, who were estimated to be able to manage six acres of cotton and eight acres of maize each per year.

Land songs, music made to match the rhythm of the work, have a long tradition in the fields, and have found their way around the world. 'Let sowing be fast, let sowing be easy … and let us finish early so we can eat by daylight', intone the Kammu women in Laos as they prepare the paddy field – the pattern of the work imposing its own, particular rhythm. The music of the cotton pickers was different, a slower beat than the faster pulse of the sugar-cane cutters, but busier than the rhythm of the tobacco harvesters. Yet many of the cotton fields were picked without music; the work carried out in enforced silence, singing and whistling being considered a distraction to the business of separating the bolls from the 'finguhs', the compartments that held the valuable white fibre.

'Way down in the bottom – where the cotton boll's a rotten; Won't get my hund'ud all day. Before I'll be beated – before I'll be cheated; I'll leave five finguhs in the boll', sang the cotton pickers of Sea Island, Georgia. The 'hund'ud' was reckoned the minimum amount a slave hand should pick in a day. Then after the picking came the weighing in, and a whipping for anyone who failed to meet their quota.

The cotton field was a place of tyranny for the black slave. It was hard on the soil too. By 1885, with the topsoil in Georgia seriously damaged by the cotton fields, cotton growers spread west into Louisiana, Arkansas, Texas and north up the Mississippi River. These were Native American territories, but their inhabitants had no hope of holding their ground against the economics of King Cotton. Their lands were expropriated and their people moved out in a series of forced migrations that killed thousands.

UPLAND COTTON

Name: Upland cotton
(*Gossypium hirsutum*)

What it's like: The yellow, cream or rose cotton flower is as attractive as those of the other members of this family, which includes the hibiscus and the hollyhock.

A perennial plant in the wild – it is thought to have originated in Brazil – commercial varieties are grown as short-stemmed annuals, which makes them easier to harvest by machine. After pollination and flowering, the plant heads develop bolls that contain white cotton fibre, used to make cloth; these are attached to short fuzzy fibres, or linters.

There are around 39 species of cotton in the genus *Gossypium*; it was 'upland' cotton (*Gossypium hirsutum*) that came to dominate commercial production and that now accounts for around 95 per cent of the world's cotton crop.

Cotton is the most important non-food crop in the world, with the seed being used in the manufacture of soap, margarine and cooking oil, and the thread producing cloth, paper, nappies, bandages and a host of other domestic goods. The linter fibres are used in gunpowder, sausage skin, cellophane, nail varnish, plastic, ice cream, chewing gum and make-up.

Where it's grown: China, India, Pakistan, Africa and the United States, where cotton occupies more fields than any other crop.

'Way down in the bottom –
where the cotton boll's a rotten;
Won't get my hund'ud all day.
Before I'll be beated – before I'll be cheated;
I'll leave five finguhs in the boll.'

Cotton pickers' song from Sea Island, Georgia, quoted in *Swing the Sickle for the Harvest Is Ripe* by Daina Ramey Berry

The abolition of slavery hit the United States' southern cotton fields hard and saw production shift to other parts of the world including Asia and West Africa, where cotton had been first cultivated in the 19th century. (The United States is now the third-largest cotton exporter behind China and India.) Mechanisation and chemical pesticides would eventually save the American cotton crop and keep under control one of the world's most expensive pests, the boll weevil. This beetle reached the American cotton fields from Mexico in the 1890s and within 30 years had become an endemic problem, costing an estimated U.S. $300 million a year, much of it spent on aggressive pesticides. Cotton is a natural fabric, yet more chemical controls are used on cotton than any other crop – while cotton accounts for less than 3 per cent of the world's farmed land, it consumes about a quarter of the world's pesticides.

Milpa Fields

'We shall be inclined to pronounce the voyage that led the way to this New World as the most epoch-making event of all that have occurred since the birth of Christ,' intoned John Fiske in 1891 in his two-volume work *The American Revolution*. In many ways Fiske was right, not least when it comes to this voyage's impact upon the fields of the New World.

Hollywood's mid-20th-century portrayals of Native Americans as whooping savages who relished attacking wagon trains and scalping their occupants was as wildly inaccurate as some of the 17th-century fictions surrounding the Italian explorer Christopher Columbus. Yet the fate of the Native Americans and their fields was inextricably linked to Columbus's arrival. The Muslims were being driven out of Spain in the same year, 1492, that the Genoese explorer Columbus set sail with three ships, *Niña, Santa Maria* and *Pinta*, in search of the fabled maritime shortcut to China and the East Indies. Instead he made landfall in the Bahamas, the first European to reach the Americas since the Vikings: 'The world is small', he remarked with surprise, convinced that he had reached Asia, and named this first footfall in the Americas as the West Indies to distinguish them from the East Indies. Similarly he dubbed the native people 'Indians' because he assumed they were native to the Indies. (The Italian who was able to demonstrate that Columbus had actually found a fourth continent, Amerigo Vespucci, would have the New World named after him.)

It may not have matched up to John Fiske's estimation; however, Columbus's arrival did shift the balance of economic power in favour of the West and away from China; it altered the balance of the world's faiths as the growing

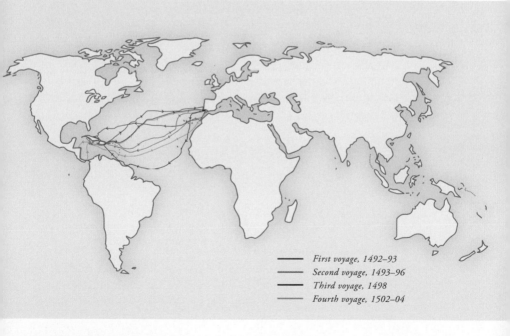

———— *First voyage, 1492–93*
———— *Second voyage, 1493–96*
———— *Third voyage, 1498*
———— *Fourth voyage, 1502–04*

The four voyages of Christopher Columbus to the New World. The New World was first sighted by Rodrigo de Triana on 12 October, 1492, from aboard the caravel *Pinta*.

number of Americans bolstered the ranks of Christianity; and it even altered the course of evolution – until the exchange of people, plants and animals across the Atlantic, animal life had been developing along separate evolutionary lines.

The discovery of the 'New World' also heralded the end for the indigenous agrarian way of life. When Columbus landed, the people he found were still working the *milpa* ('field' in the Aztec or Nahuatl language) – a patch of cleared forest or jungle where farmers planted complementary crops. American Indians traditionally performed a respectful ritual when they sowed their maize (corn). Sensibly burying a fish beneath the seed to act as a slow-release fertiliser, and sowing their lima beans around the plants – they used the maize stems for support – they then waited for the cobs to ripen. The first were ceremonially cut and baked in the embers of the fire during the Green Corn Festival.

Maize, lacking sufficient protein, needs to be balanced with other foods. So the milpa was also used to grow sweet potatoes, avocados, melons, tomatoes, squash, beans and chilies. Under such intensive cultivation the milpa's fertility was quickly exhausted and the field would then be rested – one cycle recommended two years of cultivation and eight years of fallow. Otherwise the milpa was simply abandoned to the wilds and a new clearing created.

After Columbus's arrival the fight for the fields of the New World involved little of either the sword or the ploughshare, although both were employed, the first with savagery, the second with impunity. Instead, most of the Native Americans fell ill and died. The white settlers brought with them diseases that saw the native population plummet from an estimated five million to just half a million. 'They die like rotted sheep', wrote William Bradford, one of the founding Pilgrim Fathers, when an epidemic of smallpox slaughtered the natives, but left the Pilgrims, who had built up an immunity, untouched. It prompted one cleric to declare, 'The Lord hath cleared our title', as the new landowners systematically settled the land.

Today's New World is a very different place. Now millions routinely begin their day with a bowl of cornflakes and end it with a beef steak, the fields of the Americas produce an astonishing range of food, and feed an extraordinary number of people. But where the little milpa once thrived, the new fields are under pressure.

The new settlers renamed the land and changed the face of the fields. One district was renamed Misiones by Jesuit missionaries and is still covered by a sub-tropical forest that is home to monkeys, alligators and the bright-billed toucan. Neighbouring Entre Rios, where the trees were felled and the land replanted, is covered with pastureland stretching into Uruguay. The region was named La Mesopotamia after the once-fertile region of the Middle East that also lay between two great rivers, in this case the Paraná and the Uruguay, and in common with the old country its land is under agricultural pressure to produce more and more. Argentina relies on its tobacco, citrus, rice and soya-bean crops and on the raising of sheep, poultry and beef cattle. According to the United Nations Food and Agriculture Organisation, around 40 million acres (16 million hectares) of forest were lost to farming between the 1980s and 2000.

Slash and Burn

Slash-and-burn farming is a more benign use of land than its name implies. Subsistence farmers in places as far apart as Brazil, the Congo and Indonesia have been raising crops of cassava and sweet potatoes from the ashes of forest fires for centuries.

Using machetes or pangas, a clearing is hacked from the forest and the bush is fired. The resulting ash fertilises the soil sufficiently for a few bountiful years until fertility dips again and the farmers – one in 25 across the world – move on. Left fallow for long enough, the land will return to forest for future use by slash-and-burn farmers, who apply no artificial fertilisers and rarely use anything other than hand power to create these temporary fields. Provided that the population remains stable and land use is kept to a low level, the slash-and-burn system can be a sustainable form of farming.

What may have started as slash-and-burn clearings are now curious, charcoal-rich patches of land, the *terra preta do indio*, or 'black Indian earth', which have been discovered by archaeologists. Dating back long before the arrival of Columbus, these deep, fertile pockets of dark soil resemble the lovingly tended vegetable plots of old Europe, fertilised year after year with compost and manure. (One of the first to record them was a Dutch soil scientist, Wim Sombroek, who was struck by their similarity to the *plaggen*, rich agricultural soil pockets created over the centuries in parts of Europe by careful husbandry.)

These patches of *terra preta do indio* have been found not only in South America's Ecuador and Peru, but also in West Africa, in Benin and Liberia, and in the savannahs of South Africa, where local farmers exploit them for crops of papaya and mango that grow three times as fast as those on surrounding soils. The soil still holds some strange secrets.

OPIUM POPPY

Name: Opium poppy
(*Papaver somniferum*)

What it's like: A member of the same family as the field (also corn or scarlet) poppy (*Papaver rhoeas*), the opium poppy grows to over 1 metre (3 feet) high and has striking white, pink, red or purple-blue blooms. The drug is extracted from the immature seed head and dried, although the pale yellow oil taken from the seeds is non-narcotic and used for cooking.

Opium was celebrated by the ancient Greeks for its calming, medicinal qualities. Opium and its derivative laudanum were popular recreational drugs for many 19th-century literary figures including the author Thomas De Quincey (1785–1859). He became a household name when, in 1821, he published the *Confessions of an English Opium Eater*, a wild and creative account of his years of addiction to the drug which, at the time, was commonly used by politicians, preachers and nursing mothers alike.

Ironically, the products of the poppy have the power to both calm and kill. In 1805 morphine was isolated by Friedrich Wilhelm Sertürner, who named his discovery after Morpheus, the Greek god of dreams. Morphine is one of medicine's most effective painkillers while heroin, which is derived from morphine and was marketed at the end of the 19th century as a non-addictive morphine substitute, is a highly addictive drug.

Where it's grown: Native to southeast Europe and western Asia, the opium poppy is now grown in Turkey and across the East. The consequences of its cultivation are particularly problematic in countries such as Afghanistan, India, Myanmar and Thailand.

Opium Fields

The Chinese pictogram for the field bears a striking similarity to that for the mind, but in the early part of the 20th century the minds of over a quarter of all grown men in China were muddled by the products of the poppy fields. They were hooked on opium.

The world has not seen such levels of mass addiction before or since: not even the opium derivative, heroin, discovered in 1874 and responsible for enslaving so many young men and women in the West, has matched the chaos caused by widespread opium addiction in China. Yet the source of this addiction lay, not in the fields of China, but in India. And the cartels that controlled the opiate supplies and spread misery among both the growers in India and the consumers in China were the clandestine representatives of Western nations including Britain, France and America.

The problem could be traced back to the 1490s when Vasco da Gama sailed around the Cape of Good Hope and opened the first sea trade routes between East and West. Initially the Portuguese and Spanish monopolised the business, but China was to prove a reluctant trading partner. The nation enjoyed its silks, porcelains, and above all its tea, and while it welcomed some silver in exchange, the self-contained Chinese wanted virtually nothing else from the West.

In 1793 a British dignitary, Lord Macartney, visited China hoping to wheedle some lucrative trading concessions out of China's Manchu leaders. However, China did not regard itself as an 'Eastern' nation: its dynasty, independent and self-sufficient, sat at the centre of the world, safe, stable and secure, and with no desire for foreign interference. One Chinese delegate even commiserated with Macartney for 'the lonely remoteness of your island, cut off from the world by intervening wastes of sea.' Yet within 50 years the social system that had ruled China for thousands of years would be brought to its knees by foreign fields of poppies.

The Western nations, frustrated by China's resistance to the profitable possibilities of trade, created their own: they introduced tobacco from Portugal's Brazilian fields and opium from Bengal. It proved an intoxicating combination.

Opium is harvested by scoring the surface of the ripening poppy head in the evening and then collecting the milky-white sap that oozes from the scars by morning: raw opium. The sap is scraped from the plant, rolled into pellets, and dried in the sun. Raw opium contains morphine, codeine and thebaine, alkaloids that relieve pain and induce a deep drowsiness. It has been exploited for at least 6,000 years. The Greeks and Romans were familiar with it – Homer mentions it in his *Odyssey* – as were the literary figures of 19th-century England: Wilkie Collins, Samuel Taylor Coleridge, Charles Dickens and Percy Bysshe Shelley.

Arab merchants had first brought opium overland to China in the East, and Europe in the West. When Britain took possession of Bengal's opium fields after Robert Clive defeated the Indian Mogul armies at Plassey in 1757 – Clive later became an opium addict himself – it took control of China's main source of illicit opium. The British East India Company, under the protection of its government, organised the business of buying and processing the drug in India – the growers were virtually enslaved to the company. The British East India Company absolved itself of direct responsibility for actually smuggling the drug into China. Instead it used freelance agents equipped with fast ships designed to evade Chinese officials who refused to be bribed into submission.

As long as the East India Company controlled the supply of opium, it also controlled the price. But profits were enormous and soon rival supplies of Malwa opium were arriving from western India and, in American boats, from Turkey. As this increased competition caused the street price of opium to fall in China, the addiction rate began to rise.

The Chinese authorities still resisted, however. Imperial orders banning opium smoking had been made as far back as 1729, and again in 1799, but it was too late to stop the drug undermining almost every aspect of Chinese life. And to underline its inalienable right to trade, Britain, in the early 1840s and again in 1856, flexed its military muscles and sent gunboats and soldiers in to defeat the ill-equipped Chinese in the two Opium Wars. The amount of opium entering China rose after each conflict.

By now China's population had risen to 430 million. The hitherto stable rule of the Qing dynasty (which lasted from 1644 to 1911) and their Manchurian leaders had helped the nation to prosper, but also triggered a population boom. Pressure on the peasants to feed so many mouths was intense, and between 1850 and 1864 the Taiping revolutionaries seized farmland, banning private ownership, grading the fields according to quality, and working them in communal plots. It was the peasants' first taste of communism.

In order to defeat the revolutionaries, the weakened Manchu government was compelled to turn to the foreign powers it so despised, France, the United States and Britain, for arms and aid. And they were forced to make a crippling concession: to legalise the import of opium.

Opium addiction eventually permeated every level of society and cost China its sovereignty. By the end of the 19th century China was a nation in decline. The last emperor, the child Pu-Yi, abdicated in 1912. He would die in 1967 working as a humble archivist during yet another peasant movement, the Cultural Revolution that hauled the nation into the 20th century.

After the Second World War, opium addiction was brought under control in China, but the field trade in heroin continues in Mexico and in Afghanistan – which produces 90 per cent of the world's opium. Efforts to stop the heroin trade have varied from destroying the crops to paying farmers to switch to other crops. Although small amounts of opium can be grown for medicinal rather than narcotic purposes, one solution could lie with the pomegranate. Afghanistan grows some of the world's best pomegranates, but 30 years of war have decimated its orchards. In 2008 plans were revealed to re-establish pomegranate orchards, which take five years to mature. Thereafter they could earn the farmer twice the income promised by the equivalent field of opium poppies.

Collective Fields

The utopian vision of cheerful workers striding out in the new dawn to farm the collective fields was first put forward by 19th-century idealists such as the philanthropist and textile-mill owner Robert Owen, Étienne Cabet who founded the Icaria community at Corning, Iowa, and Charles Fourier, whose ideas inspired the foundation of communities such as La Réunion, Texas.

Each advocated his own theories on the collective field, but the *kibbutz* (from the Hebrew for 'gathering'), first founded in the new state of Israel by a group of Russian pioneers in 1909, proved to be one of its more successful incarnations. On the kibbutz a mother would place her children in communal care before setting out, armed with a rifle, to farm the communal fields. In the troubled state of Israel, under constant threat of attack from its neighbours, the kibbutz at the height of its popularity combined the attributes of the farm with the security of a fortress. It had three aims: to combine working the land with industrial production – running a stacking and packing yard alongside the olive, avocado and orange fields, for example; to raise the kibbutz children together; and to act as a watch post in time of trouble.

By 1965 there were 230 kibbutzim, some up to a thousand strong, and while the 80,000 Israelis who lived in the kibbutzim represented only 5 per cent of the population, the system was judged to work well. In fact, in the 1990s about half the people who worked the land still lived in the kibbutzim or the co-operative *moshavim*.

The USSR's full-scale social experiment with field collectives was disastrous by comparison. In 1929 'Uncle' Joe Stalin, the bear-like premier of the Soviet Union, celebrated his 50th birthday. The number of peasants then working the fields of the Soviet Union was around 26 million. By the time he was 58, the number had fallen to 19 million since Stalin had set out to 'systematically eliminate' capitalists from agriculture and to collectivise the fields.

In other Eastern European countries such as Poland and the former Yugoslavia, collectivisation was tried and then abandoned. Stalin, however, put field reform in the front line for change and achieved it using draconian powers.

'It is essential that the operations of removal of both members of the deportee's family and its head shall be carried out simultaneously, without notifying them of the separation confronting them.' These were the chilling instructions issued to the Soviet police responsible for dealing with the landowning *kulaks*, farmers who had learned to manage the land, yet were first in the firing line.

A first-category kulak was a farmer who hired in labour, sold goods at market and loaned money. Most of these 'class enemies' were taken out of their farms and shot. Those who escaped summary execution were deported to labour camps. A second-category kulak could expect to be deported for 'resettlement' in the north, Siberia, the Urals and Kazakhstan. Those of the third category were simply deprived of their goods and chattels.

This de-kulakisation was responsible for the slaughter of millions – although no one knows precisely how many – while the remaining peasants were instructed to make use of 'neglected land', to obtain machines and tractors, and to double productivity. They were also told to hand over their farm animals to the state. Instead they routinely butchered the stock, salted down what they could keep for themselves, and sold the rest on the black market. In the opening years of collectivisation, this led to the destruction of a quarter of the farm animals, an unforeseen consequence of field reform that left the world's largest nation struggling to recover for the next 20 years.

Meanwhile, the peasantry reluctantly signed up to the *kolkhozi*, the farm collectives, or the *sovkhosi*, the state-owned farms. Propaganda films showed happy young women, their leather jackets and boots encrusted with good Soviet mud, delivering Russian tractors to the kolkhozi while their leader exhorted his people to even greater agricultural production. But the reality was quite different: a state-run agricultural system that had failed its people and was responsible for food shortages and a flourishing black market. Stalin died in 1953 and the Soviet Union went through a gradual process of change. In the 1980s, as the kolkhozi were quietly abandoned, a new leader emerged, Mikhail Gorbachev, himself the son of a kulak.

Fields of Fuel

Much of the world's wealth is founded upon the exploitation of fossil fuels. And many of the richest nations owe their wealth to fields of oil. However, the reserves they draw upon were created hundreds of millions of years ago when dead biological matter was compressed and heated as it lay buried under layers of sediment. One day these fields will run dry, and the combination of political imperatives and the environmental impact of fossil-fuel consumption means that the search is underway for alternative fuels for the world's economies.

In Brazil, fields of sugar cane are being processed to fuel a national program that has seen 90 per cent of the country's cars run on the petroleum substitute 'cane alcohol', or ethanol. Although grown at some cost to tracts of virgin Amazonian forest, this is less polluting than conventional fuels. Elsewhere, maize, sweet sorghum, beet, sweet potatoes, sugar cane and cassava are all being grown for fuel, despite fears that diverting fields to biofuel production will exacerbate existing food shortages.

Fields of fuel are nothing new, however. In the Bible, God tells Moses: 'Command the children of Israel, that they bring unto thee pure oil olive beaten for the light, to cause the lamps to burn continually' (Leviticus 24:2, King James Bible). Likewise, the Egyptians, Greeks and Romans all burned olive oil in their lamps. More recently, before the discovery of the oil field, many homes relied on the elementary lamp where a length of whittled rush, cut from the field, burned

'Command the children of Israel, that they bring unto thee pure oil olive beaten for the light, to cause the lamps to burn continually.'

Leviticus 24:2, King James Bible

in a crucible filled with vegetable oil. A popular peasant version in Ireland and Western Europe was the *cruisie*, a set of two pear-shaped vessels, one fixed above the other. The upper vessel was filled with vegetable oil, fish oil or tallow (animal fat). A wick made from a piece of twisted linen lay along the spout of the dish, and excess hot fat dripped into the collecting dish below as it burned. A common and malodorous source of fish oil was the livers of cod, seal, shark and whales; the cruisie was hung close to the hearth so that the foul smell of the oil wafted away up the chimney. The alternative was tallow candles, made from rendered animal fat, although these did not smell much better. Frugal householders often made their own candles, tipping mutton tallow into candle molds purchased from travelling tinsmiths.

Unlike tallow, beeswax and whale oil burned cleanly, but such candles were expensive. The English diarist Samuel Pepys reported in 1662: 'In Greenland they have eleven hogshead of oyle out of the tongue of a whale.' In fact, the depletion of whale stocks was a direct consequence of the need to light the home. In Pepys's time olive oil was the next best thing, not only for burning in lamps, but for treating woollen cloth and making soaps and paints. But outside the Mediterranean regions olive oil was expensive; and, just as many nations depend upon the Middle East's oil fields today, so northern Europe was once reliant on the south's olive groves. When in the 1570s Spain diverted supplies of oil away from the north to the more lucrative West Indies it triggered a price hike and increased demand for the 'olive oil of the north' – rapeseed oil.

Oil-seed millers had previously experimented with making oil from a range of crops including linseed and turnip – although in 1539 one English writer, Sir Thomas Elyot, warned against the turnip since 'it augmenteth the seed of man and provoketh carnal lust' – but rapeseed was already growing in the Netherlands by the mid-14th century and it was the Dutch farmers who showed their French, German and English neighbours how best to harvest it. And so for centuries did the humbler households rely on olive or rapeseed oil, or stinking tallow, for their light. These vegetable oils were gradually edged out by cleaner-burning oils such as coconut fat and palm oil, before the discovery in 1854 that petroleum could be used to make high-quality paraffin. By the end of the 19th century the average household was dependent on crude oil for its candles and lamps.

Rapeseed fields in the Home Counties of England, source of the 'olive oil of the north' since the 14th century when Dutch farmers began to cultivate the crop.

Flower Fields

In April and May every year fields of tulip bulbs burst into flower in the Netherlands. Over 10,000 hectares (25,000 acres) are devoted to growing 800 varieties of tulip while an equivalent area again grows other bulbs such as lilies, daffodils, irises and crocuses. The fields of the Netherlands produce around 10 billion bulbs for export and around 60 per cent of the world's cut flowers, which makes the country the third-largest exporter of agricultural produce after the United States and France.

In 1630 the 53-year-old artist Peter Paul Rubens settled down to domestic life with his new bride, the 16-year-old Hélène Fourment, at his house and studio, the Rubenshuis in Antwerp. Hélène bore him four children and in his final years Rubens made many affectionate portraits of her including *Rubens and Hélène Fourment Walking with Their Child*. Exhibited in 1633, it showed the family strolling through their garden towards the Rubenshuis with a stand of flowers in the background. One blossom in particular stands out: the tulip. A year later Holland was plunged into *Tulpenwoede*, tulip mania.

A century earlier, a European ambassador travelling in Turkey had noticed a profusion of the cup-shaped flowers growing in a Turkish garden. The tulip was originally a wild flower of Central Asia, first cultivated by the Turks around 1000 C.E. The ambassador collected specimens of what the locals called the *lalé* to take home to Vienna, but in a confusing exchange with his guide, the ambassador came away with the name 'tulip' – the guide had been likening the shape of the lalé to his turban or *tulipand*. The name, and the mania, for this distinctive bloom were born.

It took the eminent Flemish botanist Charles de L'Écluse, known as *le père de tous les beaux jardins* ('the father of all beautiful gardens'), to successfully introduce the exotic bulbs to the gardens of northern Europe and to painters including Rubens. In the 1590s L'Écluse became the director of the oldest botanical garden in Europe, the Hortus Botanicus in Leiden. He was sent some tulip bulbs by his friend Ogier de Busbecq, the ambassador to Constantinople, and he grew them, noting, as he did so, the flower's habit of breaking into variegated forms from a single colour.

Tulip fields near The Hague, Holland, paint a scene that evokes the Dutch national obsession with the tulip, which gripped the country with tulip mania in the 17th century.

It was these forms that caused such a flurry of interest and saw the tulip traded like gold. Fortunes were staked on single specimens: one dealer exchanged most of the contents of his farmyard, including oxen, pigs, sheep, the granary, the dairy, the house brewery and the wine cellar together with the household silver and a bed for a single bulb. Some families were ruined by the run on the tulip bulb. For the unfortunate L'Écluse, the *Tulpenwoede* resulted in his entire stock being stolen. The collection was subsequently said to have been used to lay the foundations for the modern Dutch tulip fields.

Failing Fields

Today around a seventh of Americans and Canadians, almost a third of all Australians and one-sixth of New Zealanders can lay claim to Irish forebears. Many of the original emigrants came from the hard-pressed regions in the west and southwest of Ireland, and most took with them little more than the old country songs and sad memories when they left for a new life overseas. The story repeated most often, the one lodged in the folk memory, was of the fields that had let them down, the lazybeds.

Fifty years before Ireland's Great Famine of the 1840s, a population of around five million was putting a severe strain on the business of scraping a living from the fields. The land around the farmsteads, or *clachan*, had once been worked as *rundale* (see Open Fields on pages 51–2) with strips passed around to give everyone a chance to work the best and the worst of the land – hence its alternative name 'changedale'.

But the 19th century saw all this changing. Now the practice of dividing inherited land among all the male heirs of a family, and subdividing pocket-handkerchief-sized fields into even more meagre off-cuts of land, pushed the field to its agricultural limits. Smallholders started planting lazybeds, raised strips of land 1 metre (3 feet) wide and bordered by a narrow trench, and often situated on low, fertile margins of the bogland.

Here in spring seed potatoes were cut in half and planted out. But by early June 1845 the sour smell of the disease, blight, was drifting across the fields. The crop was lost. In 1846 and 1848 the blight struck again. Of an estimated population of eight million in 1841 almost a million starved. Two million more were driven into the fever-ridden boats, dubbed 'coffin ships', that sailed out of Cork and Dublin, carrying their passengers to an uncertain life overseas.

Yet during the Great Famine Ireland continued to export grain to England even as its people, mostly in the south and west, were starving. In the hard decades that followed, the landlords' agents were still evicting their starving tenants.

After the Famine, inflated rents, unmanageable mortgages and systematic evictions made country living intolerable for many working people. Eventually land reforms were introduced to redistribute almost three-quarters of the land from landowner to tenant. The reforms left relatively few of the grand, old houses with surrounding estates of more than 120 hectares (300 acres) or so, and as the bankrupt owners abandoned their manor houses, many holdings were reorganised so that the fields formed a convenient series of rectangles behind the farmhouse, the so-called 'ladder farms' that are still a familiar sight in the Irish countryside. By the turn of the 20th century, changedale and the clachans had become folk memories. The failed fields, however, were never forgotten.

Potato Fields

John Worlidge in his *Systema Agriculturae* in 1669 declared: 'They [potatoes] are much used in Ireland and America as bread and may be propagated with advantage to poor people.' He was not far wrong. The people in Peru were fond of potatoes too: they had been eating them for 5,000 years and archaeological evidence suggests that they venerated the crop. Since then the potato has become one of the world's largest food crops after sugar cane, maize, wheat and rice, and the third-greatest source of protein on the globe.

But in 1795 one David Davies was predicting that 'though the potato is an excellent root, deserving to be brought into general use, yet it seems not likely that the use of it should ever be normal in the country.' It did not help that when people ate their potato raw, it often triggered eczema, then thought of as a form of leprosy. Nor that the fruit of the potato – like belladonna also a member of the family Solanaceae – was poisonous. Ignoring the virtues of the tuber, the English writer John Evelyn advocated eating potato fruit as a pickled salad. It was left to English naturalist and clergyman Gilbert White (1720–93) to point out in March 1758 that 'potatoes have prevailed in this little district ... and are much esteemed here now by the poor, who would scarce have ventured to taste them in the last reign.' It was a sign of the changing fortunes of the potato. After a famine in Prussia, the Germans reluctantly started to consume the potato: it helped that Frederick the Great sent in free potatoes, together with soldiers with

POTATO

Name: Potato
(*Solanum tuberosum*)

What it's like: Fields grow a whole range of nutritious roots and tubers including cassava or manioc, yam, sweet potatoes and sugar beet, but the potato accounts for more than half of the world's production of root crops.

The tubers are formed underground beneath a flowering bush that produces poisonous fruits. In the potato field the soil is mounded up around the plant to provide space for the subterranean tuber to multiply.

Potatoes can be divided up into waxy varieties – with delightful names such as Jaune de Holland and Blue Eigenheimer – and the more floury varieties, and come in a range of colours from blue and black to yellow, white and red – one South American species, the inedible *S. stenotomum*, is used for dyeing cloth.

In Peru the potato was *papas*, but it was also known as *pommes de terres* (earth apple) originally by French settlers in America, and *kartoffel* in German. The word *potato* (in Wales *pytatws*) originates with the mistaken idea that it was related to the sweet potato or *batata*.

Where it's grown: Except in the humid tropics, potatoes are grown almost everywhere including northern Europe and North America, with Russia and Poland producing the greatest tonnage.

orders to persuade the peasantry to try them. The grateful citizens of Offenburg, Germany, were even persuaded to erect a statue to Sir Francis Drake, holding a potato, in the town square – although the statue was removed during the Second World War when the Nazis took offence.

In France the potato was slow to catch on. When Marie Antoinette, Louis XVI's queen consort, famously suggested of her starving subjects '*Qu'ils mangent de la brioche*' ('Let them eat cake'), a French pharmacist, Antoine-Auguste Parmentier, had a better idea: '*Qu'ils mangent des pommes de terre.*' ('Let them eat potatoes.') Parmentier knew what he was talking about, having survived as a prisoner of war in Prussia on a diet of potatoes, and he was determined to introduce the famine-busting tuber to France.

The potato's cause was aided when Louis wore its white flower as a buttonhole. His courtiers fawned in admiration. The royal gourmets were further intrigued when Parmentier arranged a dinner where every course included the *pomme de terre*, or 'earth apple'. But in 1770 Parmentier dealt Gallic prejudice against the potato its *coup de grâce* when he had a field of potatoes planted at Versailles. Guards were posted ostentatiously to protect the crop, and the peasantry, as Parmentier planned, were intrigued. Under cover of darkness, the field was raided and the crop passed around. The potato had truly arrived.

In 1793, when Louis XVI was executed, French revolutionaries dug up the Tuileries gardens and planted them with potatoes. Today Parmentier is commemorated still with potato dishes such as *Hachis Parmentier*, a meal of minced beef and mashed potato. When years later the failed potato crop devastated Ireland, it prompted the garden author E. A. Bunyard to write: 'No one … will regard a potato as a mere vegetable, but rather as an instrument of destiny.'

Chapter Four

FIELD
FLORA

From pasture to paddy, from cornfield to cotton field, and from vineyard to hop yard, what defines a field is usually what grows there. And, with 10,800 different species of grass in the world, there is a lot of grassland about.

Grass: Carpeting the World

When rainfall is too low to revive arid scrub, to nourish trees, or to green the desert, grass grows. Give it a reasonably rich soil and a growing season of between 120 and 200 days, and grass positively thrives in both the tropical zones, such as South America, parts of Australia and Africa, and temperate zones, such as the southeast Australian rangeland or the Great Plains of North America.

'These are the gardens of the Desert, these; The unshorn fields, boundless and beautiful,' wrote William Cullen Bryant of the Great Plains in his 1832 poem 'The Prairies'. (The word prairie comes via the Old French *praerie* from the Latin *pratum*, meaning 'meadow'.) They covered 3 million square kilometres (1.2 million square miles) and since the 19th century, 99 per cent of this land has been turned into vast, high-yield cereal fields. The Serengeti Plains of East Africa are tiny by comparison at 25,000 square kilometres (8,900 square miles). They constitute a tropical grassland, the red, volcanic ash soils enriched by both accidental and man-made grass fires that suddenly sweep across the plains, farmed and fired by the Maasai tribes who herd their sheep, cattle and goats on the plain.

Another temperate grassland is the South American *Pampas* (from the Quechua Indian for 'flat surface'). Running east from the Andean foothills to the edge of the Atlantic Ocean, it ranges from the arid Patagonian Pampas where the icy *pampero* winds stir the blades of grass, to the rich and fertile farm settlements around Buenos Aires where the horse-mounted *gauchos*, or cowboys, run their herds of cattle to graze the plains.

There are other temperate grasslands in southeast New Zealand, southeast Australia and southern Africa and, although still smaller than the American Great Plains, the great temperate grasslands or steppes of Central Asia.

The Pampas grasslands of Chile, like the other grasslands of the world, represent a great and diverse resource for all humankind.

Characterised by their hot summers and cold winters, they stretch from the shores of the Black Sea into northeast Asia. This is one of the least populated regions of the world. Farming here is harsh and confined to grazing and raising fodder crops for cattle, sheep and goats. It is also home to the only truly wild horse, Przewalski's Horse, which is gradually being re-introduced after it had almost slipped into extinction.

On the grassland margins it is impossible to grow crops other than grass because the climate is either too cold, too dry or a relentless combination of both. Yet even here people have learned to wrest a living from the fenceless fields, grazing their sheep, goats, cattle, yaks or reindeer, which forage on lichen rather than grass. This is nomadic pastoralism, a technical description for the hard way of life in which herdspeople and their animals chase the good grazing ahead of the winter weather that finally buries the grass under the snow.

Transhumance, the business of grazing the high ground in summer and retreating to the lower slopes in winter, is a similarly sustainable way of working the grasslands. In fact, transhumance has been a traditional way of life in mountain regions across the world. Often the farmhouses, such as the Alpine *chalets* or the Pyrenean *caseríos*, have developed distinctive features that reflect this way of life: being designed to accommodate a family, their animals and the hay to feed them when the valley was locked under a blanket of snow. Spring must have come as a welcome relief after the dark months of winter.

The Basques who built their great stone and timber caseríos worked the pastures of the Pyrenees, that slice of mountains that marks the border between France and Spain, shepherding sheep – and occasionally smuggled goods – over the high passes.

The Basque homeland, *Euskal Herria*, was divided between France and Spain under the Treaty of the Pyrenees in 1659. Since then the Basques lived with the mathematical puzzle: four and three make one, a reference to the three pastoral regions in France – Labourd, Basse Navarre and Soule – and the four in Spain – Vizcaya, Alava, Guípuzcoa and the northern part of Navarre – that made up the old country. A proud and independent people as adept at sailing and whaling as at farming, the Basques speak *Euskara*, a language that embodies their independence as it is quite unrelated to either Spanish or French, with an ancestry that has eluded philologists.

Grass and sheep were central to the Basque economy. Their sheep were shorn for wool, butchered for mutton and milked for the dairy, and in the summer the shepherds moved their flocks up onto the mountain pastures. Keeping an eye out for wolves and bears, they sheltered in their dry stone hermitages, the *cabañas*, roofed with flagstones and hunkered down on the hillside out of the way of the wind. In late autumn, when the first frosts chilled the morning air, the sheep were brought down the hillside to the caseríos.

These old farmhouses – their whitewashed walls hung with necklaces of drying peppers, and a family inscription carved above their thresholds – often remained in the same family for generation upon generation. Extended down the centuries to accommodate the next young family, they were built, like the Alpine chalet, to enclose everything the family needed to see them through the winter under one roof: workshop, cart shed, stable, cattle stalls; food and fodder were stocked under the eaves.

Many of these old caseríos still stand in the Pyrenees, a testimony to the economy of grass.

Cocksfoot and Cat's Tail

Aside from pampering the lawn – the turf for which itself is sometimes raised in strange, flat fields – it's easy to take grass for granted. Yet if you look closer you will see that grasses are rich in ecological diversity, their impressive variety reflected in the very names of the different species: creeping bent, field woodrush, sweet vernal, red fescue, reed canary, wool melick, cocksfoot and meadow cat's tail. The latter, *Phleum pratense*, also goes by the curious nickname Timothy. It earned the name from an immigrant farmer, Timothy Hansen, who imported the seed from his native Norway to his new home in Carolina in 1720. Timothy was already growing in the United States, introduced by early settlers and named Herd's grass after one John Herd of New Hampshire who described it in 1711. But it was Timothy Hansen who promoted its cultivation, in spite of the assertion of one correspondent to the *American Farmer* in 1866 who insisted: 'The Timothy grass cannot under any circumstances, be adapted for pasture.'

'The Timothy grass cannot under any circumstances, be adapted for pasture.'

J. B. Killebrew, *The Grasses of Tennessee: Including Cereals and Forage Plants* in *American Farmer,* 1878

SORGHUM

Name: Sorghum
(*Sorghum bicolor*)

What it's like: An annual grass with a single stem and an inflorescence at its head composed of the densely packed sorghum grains, which are classed as millet. With over 100 different forms, the colour ranges from white and yellow to a reddish, purple brown, and local names include great millet, sorgo (grown as a source of syrup), Turkish millet, jowar (*Sorghum vulgare*, cultivated in Asia and Africa and used to make flat breads or mealies) and in Arabic as *dourra*.

First grown in Ethiopia where the early settlers applied the cereal cultivation techniques of emmer wheat to the native plant, it spread to Egypt, India and China, and was taken over to Mexico by the Spaniards. Sorghum not only feeds people and their animals, but is also fermented into a drink – *tialva* in Africa, *merisa* in Brazil. Broom sorghum was grown in 17th-century Italy for making into brooms, the stem forming the handle and the seed head the brush after the seed and chaff had been removed.

Where it's grown: The leading grain in its continent of origin, Africa, sorghum is also grown in India, China and the United States – it is the fifth most important cereal after wheat, rice, maize and barley – and as a fodder crop in Europe.

Timothy is a coarse grass, which, when ripe, looks a little like a miniature bulrush with its dense barrel of tightly packed seeds. When it's growing green, the grass provides vital grazing for livestock; when it's ripe, dry and stored as hay – or stored wet in a silage clamp – it is like cow's muesli, high in fibre and packed with nutrients. Timothy grass also provided the perfect hay fodder for horses, but since the sturdy draft horse has been replaced by the tractor, far less is grown these days.

Timothy was often sown with clover, a companion crop that was grown in the upper Midwest and Northeast of the U.S., Canada, and, apart from the coldest and hottest regions, throughout Europe. The two complementary crops grow well on rich, heavy soils – what John Baxter, author of the 1830 *Baxter's Library of Agricultural and Horticultural Knowledge*, described as 'a clayey loam; stagnant moisture is destructive of this grass' – providing rich grazing and, when the mowers sheathed their scythes and carted the hay to the rick, nutritious fodder to last the winter.

As the same author wrote: 'It is proper to take the crop when the plant is in flower, or a little after, but before the seed be perfected. When the season is dry, the crop should be taken as soon as the flowering spikes shew their antlers; but when moist and cloudy, it is more profitable to suffer a week or a fortnight to elapse before cutting for hay.' A late mowing meant that the seed head was already ripe when the hay was cut and the mower would be covered by a sparkling cloud of pollen dust – bad news indeed for the asthmatic, as Timothy grass is a common allergen.

Darwin's Meadow

Timothy grass will colonise any mowing meadow it chances upon. It was probably growing on Great Pucklands Meadow in Kent, England, in 1855 alongside typical companions such as red fescue, cowslip and the green-winged orchid. One grass in evidence that summer was the sweet vernal (*Lolium perenne*), with its green spears, the scent of which in June predicted its demise: it smelled of fresh-cut grass. When the Victorian who founded the theory of evolution, Charles Darwin, found sweet vernal he was overjoyed: 'I have just made out my first grass. Hurrah!'

Darwin, who was about to rock the scientific and religious world with the publication of his *On the Origin of Species*, lived at Down House in Kent,

England. On the day he discovered sweet vernal, Darwin was down on his knees in a hay field, counting plants. Nine years earlier he had added a small strip of woodland, rented from neighbour John Lubbock, to create what he described as his thinking path, the Sandwalk. ('Solve it by walking' or *solvitur ambulando* as the Latin proverb put it: the poet William Wordsworth similarly used a path outside his Cumbrian cottage to pace out his thoughts.)

The Sandwalk led to the sloping meadows that flanked the valley and a border of old woods. Francis Darwin, Charles's son, described the place as 'a quiet little valley losing itself in the upland country towards the edge of the Westerham Hill, with hazel coppice and larch wood, the remnants of what was once a large wood, stretching away to the Westerham road.' In 1855, armed with his eyeglass and well-thumbed flora, Darwin methodically noted down every species he could find in one of the fields, Great Pucklands Meadow.

Darwin had always judged close field work as the best way of breaking into what he called 'the awful abyss and immensity of all British Plants', and advised that 'If ever you catch quite a beginner, and want to give him a taste for Botany tell him to make a perfect list of some little field.' Researching diversity and its role in evolution, Darwin conducted his detailed examination of the 13-acre Great Pucklands Meadow beginning in June 1855. He found 142 plant species, recording the full collection in the first draft of *On the Origin of Species*.

The precise list was lost, but 150 years later a botanical survey of the meadow recorded 119 species, a remarkably small fall given the radical changes in farming methods since 1855. And in the midst of the modern survey the little green spears of the sweet vernal, the grass that prompted Darwin's 'Hurrah!', were growing still.

'a quiet little valley losing itself in the upland country towards the edge of the Westerham Hill, with hazel coppice and larch wood, the remnants of what was once a large wood, stretching away to the Westerham road.'

Francis Darwin (1848–1925), on one of his father's regular haunts

BRAMBLE

Name: Bramble, blackberry
(*Rubus fruticosus*)

What it's like: There are many different types of bramble – in fact, over 400 microspecies have been identified in Britain alone – and they are difficult to tell apart. However, the feature that marks the bramble out as a plant worth returning to every autumn is its shiny, black berry. The other notable feature is the sharp prickle that forms in lines along the biennial stems. Each year the stems arch out like spiny Slinkies, rooting where the stem tip touches the ground to create cavernous

thorny bushes that shelter and feed birds, mammals, reptiles and insects. Each stem is biennial, growing to its full length over the course of the first year, before flowering and fruiting in the second. The flowers, which are borne on branched inflorescences, have white or pink petals.

Blackberrying is a universal custom and has continued since Neolithic times – the gritty little blackberry seeds have been found in the remains of Neolithic discoveries. The fattest fruits, those at the tips of the stems, ripen first, followed by the smaller fruits behind them; however, by late autumn the final fruits are often mildewed or, so they say, touched with the Devil's spit.

Where it's grown: Native to Europe. Species within the complex have become established in many temperate regions of the world, such as Australia, New Zealand, Afghanistan, India, Indonesia, Sri Lanka, Turkey, Chile and the United States.

Great Grains

Cereals are wild grasses that have been cultivated for their seeds or grain. Three grains dominate the world's fields: maize (corn), rice and wheat. They are tradable items, as easily bought and sold on the 21st-century international commodity markets as they could be bartered at the village market.

The word 'cereal' comes from the Latin Ceres, the goddess of agriculture, but the process of the plants' domestication goes back beyond Roman times to the dawn of agriculture. This was when the gatherers of wild grain recognised its two great virtues: its richness in nutrients and its suitability for storage. Good husbandry and a rat-proof granary meant that a community need no longer watch its weaker members starve during the lean months.

When the wild grains were harvested, the farmer kept aside a bag of seed grain for the following season. Essentially this was the way that the field fed the world, and it still is now, although the nature of the husbandry varies from the ancient to the modern: in one country a subsistence farmer will walk his field, broadcasting the seed by hand, harvesting it with a sharpened sickle, and winnowing it in the wind that blows across his threshold. In another area, the seed is sown by a computer-controlled mechanical drill and harvested and threshed by machines that cost more than the first farmer could hope to earn in a lifetime.

But growing grain caused problems for the farmer. He found that, to maintain yields, the fields themselves demanded to be rested or fed with fertiliser. The Romans improved their grain crops by growing beans whose roots 'fixed' the soil with nitrogen, while the Egyptians used animal manure and plant ashes to enrich the earth.

In 1698 Martin Martin described how the St. Kildan islanders managed: the house cow was over-wintered in one room of the family home or traditional 'black house', her bedding regularly bolstered with a fresh layer of heather until, at winter's end, she could scarcely duck her head under the door. In spring, when she was turned out onto the grazing pasture, her bedding was added to ash from the turf fire, urine and the old house thatch, and spread on the fields.

Wheat harvest on the prairies of North America gathers grain with its two great virtues: it is highly nutritious and it can be kept in storage until it is needed.

Elsewhere, farmers experimented with seaweed, mouldy hay, tanner's bark, pilchards and sticklebacks, whale blubber, horn and bone, hair, woollen rags, blood, coral, urine, soot, saltpetre and household manure as fertilisers. 'Be avaricious for manure, and always keep your mind in firm conviction that your ground is in an impoverished state', advised Shirley Hibberd in the 19th-century volume *Profitable Gardening*. 'Nightmen' in towns and cities did a brisk trade carting and barging the 'night soil' out to the countryside where it was spread on the surrounding fields.

Some went to extremes: one farmer tried ploughing dead herrings into his wheat field. The crop, however, was 'so rank' it was 'laid before harvest'. During the battles of the Napoleonic Wars dead war horses would be dragged from the battlefields and sold abroad as fertiliser.

Then in the 1840s huge reserves of guano (seabird droppings) were discovered off the coast of Peru and shipped back to Europe to fertilise the fields. The guano had almost run out in 50 years, but not before it caused some changes. The number of ships that capsized when overloaded with guano prompted a British parliamentarian, Samuel Plimsoll, to come up with the simple expedient of having a loading mark, the Plimsoll Line, painted on the hulls of all maritime traffic to prevent overloading. The import of guano meanwhile forced several towns and cities to devise new systems for coping with their unwanted sewage when the agricultural market for their night soil collapsed.

Fertilisers helped improve grain yields, although how it happened was a mystery. In the 15th century, Cardinal Nicholas of Cusa tried weighing soil before and again after the crop matured. Finding little change, he concluded that water played a significant part in the process.

In the mid-1800s the German chemist Justus von Liebig, the 'father of the fertiliser industry', discovered that plants took in carbonic acid, water, ammonia, potassium, calcium, magnesium, phosphate and sulphate, and converted them into starch, sugar, fat and proteins. And, he claimed, animals that ate plants returned these vital elements to the soil in their manure. He also developed a beef extract, founding a company, Oxo, to market his beef bouillon cube. Another 19th-century German scientist, the botanist Julius Sachs, astonished the agricultural world when he grew plants without soil, 'hydroponically' in mineral-fed water.

Then, after two German chemists discovered how plants took up nitrogen, two British scientists, John Bennet Lawes (1814–1900) and Joseph Henry Gilbert (1817–1901), devised the ingredients for an 'artificial' fertiliser. Their use of nitrate of soda, nitrate of potash or sulphate of ammonia, sulphate of potash and super phosphate of lime led to some remarkable results in the field: more grain per acre.

However, higher yields meant more pests and diseases and, as with the Irish farmers' battle with potato blight (see pages 80–1), the early 19th-century farmers had to rely on natural poisons such as sulphur, derris root and nicotine to keep the bugs at bay. But by the mid-19th century farmers began to benefit from the pharmacy of chemicals developed by the dye-making industry. Over the next century chemical fertilisers, which boosted nitrogen levels in the soil, new pesticides and radically improved strains of grain from plant geneticists sent Western food yields soaring: America almost trebled its rice yields in less than a century, while Britain practically doubled its grain yields.

It all came at a cost, perhaps most famously when scientists found that the once-useful pesticide Dichlorodiphenyltrichloroethane, better known as DDT, had entered the global food chain. Farmers began to wonder what they were doing to their soils – and to themselves and their customers. The field was becoming a potentially poisonous place with residuals such as antibiotics, copper, pesticides, herbicides, cadmium and lead lurking in the land. As American author Rachel Carson warned that this unnatural war against nature would result in what she called a 'silent spring', some stopped using artificial fertilisers and pesticides and turned instead to organic farming. As the 21st century turned, a question mark hung over the oil energy required to sow, fertilise and harvest a field, given the twin threats of global warming and finite fossil-fuel reserves.

Finally, despite the huge advances in grain yields, the gulf between rich and poor, between the Western farmer's machinery and the subsistence farmer's hand tools, seemed to be widening inexorably. Counting grain yields in with the rest of the world's resources – including the products of the oil fields – around six-sevenths of the world's resources were being consumed by the wealthier half of its population. The other half was left to manage with what remained.

'Be avaricious for manure, and always keep your mind in firm conviction that your ground is in an impoverished state.'

Shirley Hibberd, *Profitable Gardening*, 19th century

Field Brewing

For centuries field barley (*Hordeum vulgare*) has been devoted to one of the basic brews of family life, beer. Since the bugs that contaminated water through pollution and dangerous drainage were killed off during the brewing process, through the course of history it has often been safer to drink beer than fresh water.

The business of drinking beer made from field grains is described in a 4,000-year-old Sumerian poem, the *Epic of Gilgamesh*: 'The shepherds ... placed beer in front of him. Enkidu knew nothing ... of drinking beer. He drank the beer ... and became expansive and sang with joy. He was elated ... and turned into a human.' People have been sharing Enkidu's elation since the Sumerians revealed how they brewed beer with sprouted and sun-dried emmer wheat and barley. This business of steeping corn in water, as the Roman Pliny the Elder noted, created 'an intoxicating drink'.

Every people from South Africa to South America have their own beer recipes: while the farmhouse brewers of Russia enjoy a tipple of 'bread beer', or *kvass*, the Zulu people brew a ceremonial *umquombothi*, a cloudy beer made from maize.

In the Middle Ages the religious orders brought a semblance of order to the European brewing business. While the ale wife catered to the domestic market – beer making was often the preserve of the mistress of the house – the monasteries concentrated on the mass market, working with the *maltster*, the grain dealer who took the farmers' barley, sprouted and dried it ready for the brewer's mash tub. From this the monks created their best, second-best and visitor-only brews (*prima melior*, *secunda* and *tertia*). The brethren were also behind the transformation from ale to beer and the arrival of a new field crop: hops.

Ale (from the Anglo Saxon *ealu*) was made with malted barley seasoned and preserved with spices and herbs such as meadowsweet. But by the 12th century hops were being added to turn ale into beer (possibly from the Latin, *bibere*, 'to drink'). The Latin *cervesia* and Spanish *cerveza* may have originated from Celtic sources, as in the Welsh *cwrwf*. Hops flavoured and preserved beer, and around 1150, the Abbess Hildegard of Bingen, Germany, was noting the use of hops or their substitute, a handful of ash leaves, to preserve the beer.

But even 'hopping' the beer did not prevent it from turning sour. In summer especially, a barrel of nutty beer could suddenly spoil, leading monks in Bavaria to try to prevent the process by fermenting the beer in chilly cellars. The colder

HOP

Name: Hop
(*Humulus lupulus*)

What it's like: Sharing the same family as the cannabis plant, *Humulus lupulus* is a tall, climbing perennial that originated in Europe and the Middle East. It is the female plant that produces the little, musk-scented, resinous cones that are used in beer making.

Hops were fermented into a drink called *symthum* in Egyptian times, but in the Middle Ages hop fields sprang up across Europe to supply the brewer.

Hop fields were characterised by their lines of tall wooden posts hung with wires and jute strings. The hop was planted in a mound of rich humus and trained to grow up the strings. In the autumn, migrant workers, who were paid on piecework rates, walked the hop yard on tall wooden stilts in order to reach and cut down the ripe vines while their family members on the ground below plucked the hops into great canvas cribs. The hops were dried in special kilns or oast houses before being packed in hessian hop pockets and sent for sale to the hop factor.

Hops can also be eaten – Russians treat the hop shoots like asparagus – while hop fibres have been processed into paper and cloth, and prized as a medicinal herb. Hops were also used medicinally to treat liver and digestive conditions.

Where it's grown: Germany is the world's leading producer of hops, accounting for a little over a third of total hop production. It is followed by America – where the vast majority of hops are grown in Washington State – China, the Czech Republic, Poland, Slovenia, the United Kingdom, Spain, Ukraine and France.

fermentation had a strange effect: instead of bubbling away on the surface of the beer, the yeasts sank to the bottom of the barrel and fermented from below. The monks christened these 'bottom-brewing' beers *Lagerbier* (*Lager* being the German for 'storehouse'), and the process was known as *lagering*.

It was these pale lagerbiers that the Bavarian master brewer Joseph Groll experimented with at Plzen, Bohemia, in 1842. His 'pils' or 'pilsner' beers would keep the barley farmer busy for years to come.

The Water of Life

Eau de vie, brandy, poteen, saki, raki, gin, tequila: the art of distilling the different field crops into a variety of potent spirits has permeated almost every culture in the world.

One of the world's most famous and best loved distillations, whiskey, was brought to Ireland by monks returning from their devotional journeys to the Holy Lands around 600 C.E. Before long the art of distilling a mixture of malted and unmalted barley, yeast and water was being copied by their compatriots in the production of what they called their *uisce beatha*, the 'water of life'. But the conquering English, when they occupied Ireland, could not pronounce what they enjoyed drinking and uisce beatha was anglicised first into *fuisce* and finally into whiskey.

In the late 1600s Sir Walter Raleigh took some 145 litres (32 gallons) of uisce beatha from the Earl of Cork's home distillery when he left on his voyage to the Americas. Here, however, people had their own particular ideas and recipes for an eau de vie. Mexicans took the leaves of the spiky cactus agave (*Agave tequilana*), cut away the leaf base, and cooked it in order to convert its raw starches into sugars. Macerated and fermented in great vats, these sugars were gradually turned into the heady spirit tequila. (Other species of agave, *A. sisalana* and *A. fourcroydes*, were meanwhile made into the hard-wearing and sun-resistant fibre sisal.)

In Newfoundland they made *Newfie screech*, distilling the sweet sediments from the bottom of barrels that had been used to carry both rum and molasses during the 18th-century trade in slaves, sugar, rum and cotton, and mixing them with grain alcohol to create their fiery eau de vie. The rye whiskey makers of the United States, meanwhile, numbered among them two Presidents: George Washington and Thomas Jefferson.

As happened during the American Prohibition, the authorities often condemned the consumption of eau de vie and outlawed the traditional farm distilleries – while being careful to license production so as to benefit from the potential tax revenues. Many old recipes were lost and forgotten.

In Ireland in the 1830s the temperance movement of Father Theobald Mathew had a formidable effect on the country stills when nearly half the adult population signed a pledge of alcoholic abstinence. Then, during the Great Famine of the 1840s, most of the country's estimated 2,000 licensed distilleries – and countless secret country stills with them – were closed down. By 1900 no more than 30 survived.

Yet although few would admit to it, the *poteen* remained an important part of country life in the late 20th century, as one 80-year-old lady from County Tyrone recalled: 'There's a nice little still at the foot of the hill, With the smoke going up to the sky …'

A 19th-century illustration of the brewing process showing the key link that alcohol has played between the crops of the fields and humankind.

RYE

Name: Rye
(*Secale cereale*)

What it's like: The ears of rye have a bristly appearance, giving the grain the look of a bearded wheat, although rye is taller (1–2 metres or 3–6 feet) and when green, has a duller, greyish-green colour.

Rye is grown for human consumption and as a forage crop. Its flour is darker than wheat flour and is used for making crisp breads and, especially in Germany, the unleavened 'black bread' that stays fresher longer than wheat bread. Rye is also used for beer making in Russia, gin in Holland, various eaux de vie in France, and whiskey in the United States. In the north Mediterranean region mountain rye (*S. montanum*) is grown for its grain.

Rye developed from wild species in Southeast Asia and seems to have been introduced to the Romans by the German and Slavic tribes they encountered.

Rye is prone to a fungal parasite, ergot, which can cause hallucinations, convulsions and death. The effects of ergot poisoning in the Middle Ages were known as St. Anthony's Fire.

Where it's grown: Rye is grown around the world, but almost 75 per cent of its production is concentrated in Russia, Poland and Germany. The crop is also produced in Latvia, Lithuania, Belarus and Ukraine, as well as Turkey, Kazakhstan, northern China, Canada, the United States and Argentina.

Bean Fields

'I will arise and go now, and go to Innisfree, And a small cabin build there, of clay and wattles made; Nine bean rows will I have there, a hive for the honeybee, And live alone in the bee-loud glade.' So wrote the Irish poet and dramatist William Butler Yeats (1865–1939) in his poem 'The Lake Isle of Innisfree', which was published in 1893.

Forty years before Yeats penned his verse, the contemplative American author Henry David Thoreau was planting up his own bean patch on the shores of Walden Pond at Concord, Massachusetts. 'What shall I learn of beans or beans of me? I cherish them, I hoe them, early and late I have an eye to them and this is my day's work.'

These two devotees of the bean were singing the praises of two different beans, separated by the breadth of the Atlantic Ocean. Thoreau, who sold his beans to buy rice, grew 'the common small white bush bean', one of over 50 varieties of *Phaseolus*, all originating from the Americas and including French, navy, flageolet, snap, haricot vert, scarlet or runner bean (*P. coccineus*) and the lima or butter bean (*P. lunatus*).

Yeats was probably hoping to plant the broad bean, or fava in America (*Vicia faba*), which, like the smaller-seeded cultivars including the field, winter, tick or horse bean, has been grown since Biblical times. In fact, bean seeds some 8,500 years old have turned up in the Middle East and the seeds may well have been introduced to northern Europe in the leather satchel of some Roman legionnaire. The plant was a valuable crop: the seed could be eaten fresh, or dried and stored for the winter months, and the plant's roots enriched the soil with extra nitrogen. The crop was so valuable that the crime of stealing beans from open fields carried the death penalty in the Middle Ages.

'What shall I learn of beans or beans of me?
I cherish them, I hoe them, early and late I have
an eye to them and this is my day's work.'

Henry David Thoreau, from *Thoreau: Walden and Other Writings*, 1862

When the European faba (or fava) bean was joined by the American bean it caused a sensation and much confusion. One 1888 European seed catalogue noted: 'The Kidney Bean, *Phaseolus vulgaris,* has been cultivated for a considerable time, but there is uncertainty as to whether it was known in Europe before the discovery of America, where the genus is strongly represented.' It was not. In reality, the kidney bean, which grows in the wilds of South America, was brought back by Spanish conquistadores along with their captured gold bullion in the 16th century. The kidney bean earned its name from its similarity to that part of the body, although in its American homeland it was the 'string bean', a reference to the stringy seams of the pod. When King Charles I's gardener, John Tradescant, collected the seed from Virginia, the 'runner bean', as it was also known, was grown merely as a decorative garden plant. But it was a better-tasting bean than the old fashioned faba or broad bean and, as the 16th-century commentator John Gerard pointed out with surprise in his 1597 *Herball,* it could be eaten 'cods and all'.

Then there were the highly favoured 'French' beans, *haricot vert*, a tender bean also eaten pod and all, and *haricot jaune*, podded and harvested for the seed. But they were not French at all: *haricot* is derived from its Aztec name, *ayacotl*, and it became known as the French bean only because of the Gallic gardeners who grew it. Another import from the Americas was the 'French' flageolet bean, so called either because it looked like a flute, or *flageolet*, or because it was a corruption of *Phaseolus*, the Latin name for a small sailing craft, a reference to its boat-like shape.

And so this confusion of beans continued down the centuries. Dutch small-holders in the 19th century developed a fondness for the early-cropping Mazagan, a bean that had migrated from the small Portuguese settlement of the same name on the Moroccan coast. (It was less well travelled than the matchbox beans of Queensland, Australia, which, being impervious to seawater, drift around the world's oceans for years.) One of Africa's better-known beans was described as a 'ground nut' because of the way in which it grew. But the African groundnut or bambara bean (*Vigna subterranea*), when added to stews, boiled and eaten as a snack, or ground into bean flour, was as versatile as that other African standby, the black-eyed bean or African cowpea (*V. unguiculata*).

The one characteristic common to all beans of the field seems to be their reputation for causing flatulence. As one traditional rhyme put it: 'Every pea has its vease [wind]; But every bean fifteen.' In fact, the poor reputation of beans dates from ancient times. Herodotus, the fifth-century B.C.E. 'father of history', reported in his

SOYA BEAN

Name: Soya bean or soybean
(*Glycine max*)

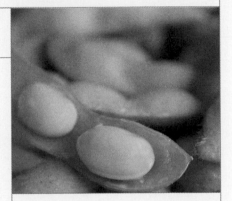

What it's like: Soya beans can grow along the ground or stand up to 2 metres (6.5 feet) high. The bean pods are grown in clusters and each produces two to four seeds. The plant's pods, leaves and stems are covered in fine hairs.

The dried beans vary in colour from white, black and brown to yellow, grey and red. They are rich in oil (20 per cent) and protein (40 per cent) and most of the soya crop is devoted to oil, the leftover meal fed to farm animals. Some soya goes directly into food for human consumption such as soya milk, tofu and textured vegetable protein – sometimes presented to vegetarians as a meat substitute. Soya is used in processed foods, too, including ice cream, yoghurt, cheese and margarine. The beans can also be eaten green: Japan's *edamame* is made from young beans boiled in their pods and served with salt.

A favourite biotech crop, genetically modified (GM) soya beans have been grown extensively in the Americas since the 1990s, although there has been consumer resistance to the GM soya bean from several European nations.

Where it's grown: The biggest producers are the United States, Brazil, Argentina, China, India, Paraguay and Canada. Concerns have been raised about the loss of rainforest to soya fields in Brazil.

Histories that Egyptian priests considered beans to be unclean, claiming that: 'Beans moreover the Egyptians do not at all sow in their land, and those which grow they neither eat raw nor boil for food; nay the priests do not endure even to look upon them, thinking this to be an unclean kind of pulse.'

Perhaps the most famous bean hater of all was the sixth-century B.C.E. Greek mathematician Pythagoras, who Diogenes Laërtius reports forbade his followers from beans on the basis that 'One should abstain from fava beans, since they are full of wind and take part in the soul, and if one abstains from them one's stomach will be less noisy and one's dreams will be less oppressive and calmer.'

Fields of Soya

Every nation had a bean to boast about. In India it was the mung bean, but for China and Japan the national bean was the soya or *dadou* (literally the 'great bean'). The Chinese have been cultivating the protein- and calcium-rich bean at least since the western Chou dynasty that ended in 770 B.C.E. It proved to be a useful vegetable and one that provided millions with a healthy, meat-free diet. Its importance can been seen in the variety of poetic names it was given, such as Large Jewel, Flowery Eyebrow, Brings Treasure, White Spirit of the Wind and Child of the White Crane.

While China's neighbours to the west, the Tatars, milked animals to provide their dairy products, the Chinese made 'milk' by crushing the soya bean and mixing it with chalk-free water. They roasted and toasted the bean and, after removing the outer skin, ground it down for flour. And if some highborn Chinese were inclined to dismiss them as 'coolie food', bean sprouts nevertheless provided a healthy, vitamin-rich salad for everyone else.

The Japanese farmer grew soya beans for soy sauce (*shoyu*), dairy-free cheese (*daizu* or *tofu*), and the staple paste that forms the basis of many sauces and soups (*miso*). When they developed *shoyu*, made from soya beans salted in oil, it triggered a case of mistaken identity. In the 1700s Dutch missionaries arrived in Japan and discovered the pale bean. Mistaking *shoyu* for the name of the bean itself they sent samples of what they pronounced 'soya' home. The benevolent bean went forth and multiplied.

A Breton onion field from where the harvest would be carried by boat and bike across the English Channel by 'onion Johnnies' in the years between the two World Wars.

In the 1900s American growers helped put the soya bean among the world's most grown vegetables along with maize, potatoes, sweet potatoes and sugar beet. The British are said to be the world's biggest bean feasters.

Surprisingly, the seemingly modern option of the soya-filled veggie burger and meat-free sausage arose over a thousand years ago. It was Buddhists in the Tang empire who first turned soya-bean curds into look-alike fish, poultry and meat.

But there has been a downside to soya production. Much of the modern global trade in soya is devoted to animal feed. Feeding animals on a protein-rich diet is a highly inefficient way to supply protein for human consumption. To make matters worse, the animal appetite for soya is causing serious environmental problems as the already shrinking Brazilian rainforests are cut back further to make way for the soya bean.

Pasta and Onions

Two familiar European stereotypes have arisen as a direct result of the field work of two nations. The first is the beaming Italian, his ample girth swathed in a chef's apron, his hands dusted with the white dust of durum flour. The second is the Frenchman in his striped vest, sailor's trousers and beret, riding a bicycle with a string of onions draped over the handlebars.

The first arose from the Italian, and now the world's, fondness for pasta. The Arab invasion of Southern Italy in the eighth century introduced African gastronomy and durum wheat to the Italians. A hard-grained wheat, durum is now grown in India, Kazakhstan, Syria, Canada, Argentina, America and Mexico, and was once the staple crop of the poor soils of Italy and southern Russia. It was too hard to make bread, but it could be ground into the grits of semolina or made into a thick paste, or *pasta*. This could be mixed with other foods such as egg and then shaped into tubes (*maceroni*, meaning 'to crush or bruise'), thin flakes (*vermicelli*, meaning 'little worms' and *capellini*, meaning 'little hairs') and strings (*spaghetti*, meaning 'little cords') that could be dried and rehydrated when it was time to cook them.

Claims that Marco Polo brought pasta to the Italian table at the end of the 13th century, by introducing the Mediterraneans to Chinese noodles, were refuted by Italians who maintained that if pasta came from anywhere it was the durum-wheat-based *lagane*. (Could this have been the forerunner of lasagna?) Italy's fields of durum wheat continue to supply something like 600 different types of pasta: *ditale* (thimbles), *anelli* (small rings), *crocette* (kisses), *conchiglie* (seashell-shaped), *stelle* (stars), *penne* (quills) and the butterfly-like *farfalle* – every district had its favourite.

No doubts surround the now classic combination of pasta and the South American tomato. In 1839 the first pasta and tomato recipe was published and the rest really was history.

The corresponding French stereotype was launched between the two World Wars on the northwest coast of France, in Brittany. Times were hard in the onion fields around Trégor. Then, as the women adhered to their traditional black skirts and coiffes – they could afford nothing else – the men wore their striped seamen's shirts, their Breton berets and their sailor's trousers just as their fathers and grandfathers had before them. They had no money to do otherwise.

Unlike their forefathers, however, the young men were ready to travel to earn an extra franc or two, and in late summer, as the onion crops were gathered in, the young men would borrow the family bicycle and, carrying across the handlebars as many strings of onions as they could, ride down to the fishing ports of Saint-Brieuc or Tréguier. Here they hitched a ride on the fishing boats to the English ports. The crossing, or *journée d'Albion*, brought early onions and those who became known as the 'onion Johnnies' to southern England. For the English housewife the dashing door-to-door sellers in their berets, striped shirts and sailor's pants typified not the Breton race, but all things French. Another stereotype was born out of the field.

Chapter Five

FIELD
FAUNA

Fields are full of life. No walk through a field would be complete without taking time to observe the creatures that share it with you. Of course, there is no way that we could cover the vast array of creatures in its entirety; instead this chapter concentrates on those that have had the greatest impact upon the field.

All Creatures Great and Small

On 1 April, 1764, a solar eclipse occurred. As hedgerow birds fell silent in the unsettling darkness, a mare in the Royal Stables at Windsor, England, gave birth to what was to become one of the world's more famous foals.

The foal, named naturally enough Eclipse, promised to be a winner. No accident of the farmyard, he was a true 'thoroughbred'. His bloodlines could be traced back to two famous Arabian horses, Darley Arabian and Godolphin Arabian. Eclipse was never to be yoked to a cart nor hitched to a plough, yet he would have a profound effect on the beasts burdened with these tasks.

The proud but patient Arabian, domesticated perhaps 5,000 years ago by Bedouins, is surrounded by legend. They say that every Arabian horse sprang from one or other of *Al-Khamsa*, 'the Five'. These were the loyal mares who returned, faithful if thirsty, at their master Muhammad's bidding when he turned his herd loose in the desert to search out an oasis.

The Arabian horse was tough enough to ride for three days without water, but it was fully domesticated, often sharing the Bedouin's family tent. Compared to the cargo-pulling draft or dray horse, to the plodding Belgians, Clydesdales, Percherons or Shires, the Arabian was a flighty beast, a hot-blooded sports model, better suited to the sport of kings, the horse race, than shouldering up to the plough.

Ten thousand years ago people began to appreciate the benefits of domesticating animals. People learned that, once collected in the village corral, animals and poultry could be bred, milked, shorn, bled, feathered or slaughtered as the need arose. So they began to keep their beasts together, stallions and mares, bulls and cows, rams and ewes, boars and sows, where they bred at random.

Domesticated horses on the Asian plains were the ancestors of many of the different breeds that graced the fields of the world before the Industrial Revolution.

They could be traded too. Surplus animals were driven to market for sale or exchange. Here, according to conventional wisdom, the best were to be bartered and the second-best were kept at home to be fattened up and finally killed.

Eclipse proved such practices wrong. He showed that the best ought to be kept for breeding. Furthermore the males and females should be separated, kept 'in and in' as the British breeder Robert Bakewell put it, and bred selectively.

The Bedouins were the first breeders of the Arabian horse: under their care and the demands of harsh desert life the Arabian developed great lungs and extraordinary endurance. The Bedouins had long understood the relative merits of bloodlines and had learned from experience that the fastest and the fairest should be preserved for breeding stock.

When the Arabian horse rode out into the world it was taken into Spain and Italy by Muslim settlers, into northern Europe by crusading knights, into the Russian and Polish royal households by courtiers, and into the Americas by the conquistadores. By the time the Arabian reached Britain, the selective breeding of horses was already underway after the English King Henry VIII, in 1535, ruled that any stallion under fifteen hands (60 inches or 152 centimetres), and mare under 13 hands (52 inches or 132 centimetres), was to be culled.

The father of stockbreeding was Robert Bakewell, a portly gentleman who, having studied farming methods in Europe, settled to run the family farm in Leicestershire when his father died in 1760. Three-quarters of the farm was devoted to pasture, which he assiduously improved, and the remainder to arable land. When it came to his stock, Bakewell decided to separate the males from the females and to breed only from the beasts that carried the characteristics he considered worth improving. Many modern breeds of field animals date from his time. The practice influenced not only animal breeders, but also men of science such as Charles Darwin, whose conclusions on natural selection developed directly from his reflections on Bakewell and thoroughbred horse breeding.

Eclipse died in 1789, but not before he had sired 335 champions. Within his 25-year lifespan the lessons of selective breeding changed the keeping and marketing of livestock: from now on, the runts and remainders were sent for slaughter. The best of the beasts were separated off in their fields.

British stockmen would claim later that during the 18th and 19th centuries, of the 20 or more breeds of cattle, horses, sheep and pigs that made a major impact on the field the only animals bred to perfection outside their islands were the Dutch Holstein, Friesland or Friesian cows, the Normandy Percheron horse and the Spanish Merino sheep. They were right.

BARLEY

Name: Barley
(*Hordeum vulgare*)

What it's like: Easy to identify by the beard on its ears of corn, barley grows on a tall stalk; the ears of grain branch out either side in opposing pairs of grain – two-row – or the less common six-row, in opposing sets of three.

The grain is used as animal feed and in the manufacture of bread and beer. The two-row barley is traditionally used in German beers and English ales, the six-row being more common in American, lager-style beers (see pages 98–100).

Non-alcoholic drinks such as barley water and *mugicha* – popular in Korea and Japan – are also made from unhulled barley, while the grain is used in soups and stews, particularly in Eastern Europe, and as a coffee substitute. In Tibet barley, ground into tsampa flour, is an important source of food.

Pearling or dehulling produces pearl barley, which can be milled into flour or turned into grits or flakes similar to oatmeal.

Where it's grown: Barley, like emmer wheat, was born out of ancient Egypt, but now it is grown across the world. Russia is the largest producer, accounting for around one-eighth of the world's production. Canada, the United States, Germany, France, Ukraine and the United Kingdom are also major producers. Barley is also sown as a winter crop in warmer places such as Australia.

Cattle

There are millions of milking cows and water buffalo in the world and a lot of nimble fingers. For, although Dr. De Laval's automatic milking machine steadily swept across the globe since he introduced it in 1904 – Anna Baldwin patented a milking machine in America in 1879, but it was not a success – dairy animals were still, as one writer put it, 'an affair of the household'.

Since it was the women who usually did the milking, the dairy breeds favoured by the dextrous housewives were those animals with small teats such as the Ayrshires of southwest Scotland, which, due to their hardiness, can now be found being milked everywhere from Norway to Nicaragua.

Of all the fruits of the field, milk was the most perishable. It also became the most important commodity sold by English farmers. As cities expanded, the field cow and the backstreet dairy parlour became a feature of every town. Typical of the entrepreneurs of the time was one Edward Matthews. He had emigrated to America in 1833; but, having failed to make his fortune, he returned to the English Midlands in 1869 where he bought a cow, Old Brownie, for £14 12s 6d. Twice daily he milked her and carried the milk round to his Victorian neighbours with a churn in a wheelbarrow. His business grew. By the turn of the 20th century his sons were running a milk shop and a herd of 80 cows. Every morning at six o'clock a dozen men would take their three-legged stools and begin hand-milking. The milk was still sold street by street, but now from the backs of a fleet of horse-drawn carts.

Different dairy breeds swung in and out of fashion as Mr. Matthews sold his milk: when the best cheese was coming from Holland, the bulky, black-and-white Friesian – able to eat its weight in grass in a week, and these days capable of producing over 7,655 litres (2,000 gallons) a year – dominated the market. When it was the turn of the English cheddars, the doe-faced, brown-and-white Ayrshires were back in favour. In a subsistence economy it made more sense to keep cows for the dairy than for the butcher's poleaxe. But as nations become richer, most demand more meat.

But Europe lacked the wide-open spaces that beef cattle required. In South Africa diseases such as *rinderpest*, spread to cattle from wild antelope and giraffes,

A Swiss cow heads for the milking parlour, but milk was once not the ubiquitous product it is today; transport and storage issues had to be resolved before it was available to everyone.

held ranching back. But the plains of North America, South America and Australia proved perfect. Ranchers raised their beef cattle and paid their restless drovers, cowboys and gauchos to drive the beasts to market until railways and refrigeration offered a cheaper alternative.

Each breed had a particular claim to fame. Scotland's most famous, the Aberdeen Angus, was shipped to Australia in the 1850s, and to New Zealand, Canada, South America and southern Africa – today there are some 50 million around the world. However, following Mr. Bakewell's example, the ranchers also improved upon their imported stock and when a farmer in the Upper Murray River Valley in Victoria, Australia, bred a black Aberdeen Angus with a short-horn cow, the Murray grey was born, and has since been exported around the world, as well as back to the counties of Aberdeenshire and Angus.

Some breeds arrived by accident. The Lincoln Red was already established in Australia, South Africa, Brazil and Argentina, when, in 1959, a consignment bound for Cuba was marooned in Canada because of the Cuban revolution. Sold off locally, they thrived on Canada's grasslands. The beasts of North and South America and Australia eventually became the main source of the world's beef.

The White Faces

As far as pulling power was concerned, the ox was once judged superior to the horse. This was not surprising, since it could be sold as meat at the end of its working life and cost half as much to keep.

A farmer with a reputation for breeding oxen that fattened up well when their days before the plough had ended was Richard Tompkins of Herefordshire, England. In the early 1700s one of his cows, Silver, bore a calf. Tompkins, in his will, left the 'cow called Silver and her calf' to his six-year-old son, Benjamin.

'The bull is quieter than a lamb, but if he wants to go through a gate he'll go through 'tho the gate be closed.'

An anonymous stockman

Benjamin named the calf Silver after its mother and, with two cows he bought from a village neighbour, eventually began to breed Hereford cattle. The breed made quiet progress in the muddy fields near the Welsh border.

Tompkins was never to know that he had bred a creature with branding almost as good as John Deere tractors – Texan cattlemen still refer to their white dress shirts as their 'Herefords', a reference to the steer's trademark white face – and an animal that would amble amiably from the shafts of the plough to the slaughterhouses that fed the world's porterhouses.

A century and a half later there were extraordinary scenes on another Herefordshire farm, Stocktonbury, when the late owner's stock of Hereford cattle were put up for sale. Bowler-hatted buyers stood ten deep on the wagons that surrounded the improvised sale ring, craning their necks for a glimpse of a famous, thickset bull with its fine pair of curving horns, Lord Wilton. In the 1870s, one of Lord Wilton's offspring, Ancient Briton, swaggered into the show ring at the Illinois County Fair and swept the prize board, continuing its tour of victory through Iowa, Sioux City, Nebraska and St. Louis. In the wake of its ponderous backside Ancient Briton helped create the United States' beef magnates, for when the beefburger was invented in the 1890s it was mostly Hereford meat that filled it.

By 1884, the day of the Stocktonbury sale, the prices paid for Herefordshire bulls had risen to around £800 due to intense interest from American ranchers. They were looking for breeds that would improve their Spanish longhorn cattle and they were much taken with the Hereford, after Henry Clay of Kentucky had imported two pairs of Herefords in 1817 on the back of rumours that the animal was immune to the ravages of milk-fever disease. The animal also proved to be a gentle giant. According to one stockman, 'The bull is quieter than a lamb, but if he wants to go through a gate he'll go through 'tho the gate be closed.' Strength was his greatest asset, and on his home territory it was not unusual to find a bemused bull wandering through the village with the remains of a field gate impaled on his impatient horns.

The animal had stamina too. In 1942 a shipload of Herefords was torpedoed by a German submarine in the Atlantic, but two of the surviving steers swam slowly back to Ireland. It was this kind of resilience that saw these burly-bodied beasts stand up to, and survive, one of America's worst ever winters in 1889.

The Herefords would go on to take over the land of the dispossessed Native Americans and the 50 million buffaloes that once roamed the Great Plains. They would transform the savannahs of Argentina, New South Wales and South

Africa, and by the mid-20th century, with over 30 million registered cattle in 25 countries, their numbers – and methane-producing by-products – were judged to pose a threat to the global climate.

When Lord Wilton lumbered into the Stocktonbury sale ring, there were worries that the noble beast would be sold abroad and lost to Britain. One local breeder instructed his farm manager to bid high, but once bidding began it was an American, one Mr. Vaughan of Indiana, who showed the keenest interest, waving a telegram in the air, evidence, he said, of his financial backers. Offers passed the £800 mark and rose to £1,000. Then £2,000. Then £3,000. Finally, mopping his brow, the auctioneer brought the gavel down on a closing price almost five times the previous record, £3,990 to a smiling Mr. Vaughan. Champagne flowed, the stockman was presented with a cheque for 35 guineas, and the proud possessor of Lord Wilton posed for his photograph in front of the national newsmen.

But that evening the mysterious Mr. Vaughan disappeared. Lord Wilton was resold the following day for a more modest £1,000.

Heavy Horses

La Perche in Normandy, France, is one of the oldest horse-breeding regions in the world and it was here that the thunderously solid Flemish draft horse was bred with lighter Arabian stock. It is still not clear whether the draft horse arrived with Roman invasion forces or originated as part of the spoils of war after the defeat of Abd al-Rahman's Moorish forces by the French. But the heavy horse, later crossbred with stallions from Spain's Andalucia, resulted, in 1823, in a horse named Jean Le Blanc, the first of the mighty *Percherons*.

The La Perche Percheron was exported to North and South America, Britain and Canada as the demand grew for heavy horses that could work the fields. Apart from southern Africa, where the draft horse was unable to withstand the climate – which is why few African farmers had recourse to the plough – almost every country had its workhorse. Local breeds proved too light for the field work and the demand for dray horses for field work and haulage grew.

Britain's livestock-breeding program had produced three classics: the Suffolk punch, traceable, it was said, to a five-year-old light chestnut advertised for sale in a local Suffolk newspaper in 1773, as 'vanners', popular for hauling light goods; the Lanarkshire Clydesdale, another solid, road-haulage breed heavily influenced by imported Flemish stock; and the heavy black horse. The heavy black was another of Bakewell's triumphs: he had imported breeding stock from the Low Countries to improve the heavy, later renamed the shire horse.

Demand for strong drays was constantly frustrated by a shortage of stallions, since the farmer could raise a better price for a young foal that was castrated and reared as a working gelding than he could raising his foal as a stallion. This niche was filled by the travelling stallion – the arrival of which on a farm in spring was an awesome occasion. As his great metal shoes crashed across the farmyard, farm dogs were locked up and girls of a sensitive disposition were ushered into the farmhouse. Consummation with the mare was brief, dramatic and accompanied by much finger-crossing by the stallion's handler.

Dray horses were mighty animals, and millions were still in harness when Europe's First World War delivered a devastating blow to their ranks. Half a million died on the battlefields of France, and in the years it took to salvage the stock, tractors and trucks had set a seal on their future.

One group of heavy horses, however, did survive. Gypsies relied on their animals to pull the family home from farm to farm as they planted, hoed and harvested the field crops. Thanks to their skill not only in handling the horses, but in breeding methods, Gypsy horse fairs lasted into the 21st century.

A 19th-century English illustration depicts a farmer ploughing a field, the plough being drawn by a pair of heavy horses and guided by hand.

Sheep

'If it wasn't for the weavers what would you do? You wouldn't have the cloth that's made of wool; You wouldn't have a coat neither black nor blue, If it wasn't for the work of the weavers.' So runs the traditional weaver's song. But if it was not for a small, unpromising herd animal from the Middle East, there would have been no wool with which to weave.

Without sheep the course of history could have been very different: there would have been no money to send Columbus on his American voyage; Europe would have avoided one of its most serious economic collapses; and the Industrial Revolution would have been delayed.

Sheep are often derided as simple-minded creatures. 'The sheep is frightened at everything,' complained William Cobbett, in his *Cottage Economy* of 1822, adding: 'The sheep is done by the time they are about six years old; for they lose their teeth.' According to hill farmers the sheep has two aims in life: to break a leg or fall down dead. Yet sheep survive. In the suffocating heat of midsummer in the Adriatic, local sheep scrounge a living, grazing the aromatic sage bushes – their milk produces some distinctive local cheeses. Meanwhile, when the snow falls and strong winds heap it into drifts on the Cumbrian fells in the northwest of England, it is the old ewe that leads the herd to the safest place to await rescue by the shepherd. This capacity to survive and yield meat, milk and wool has made sheep key to the economies of many nations.

The first sheep were brought in from the wilds of the Fertile Crescent around 10,000 years ago, and from around 3500 B.C.E. the arts of spinning and weaving spread across Europe. Wool was the first commodity to merit an international trade of its own. Romans took their sheep north and into Spain and North Africa. Greek weavers were enslaved and taken to Italy by the Normans in the 11th century, and by the 12th century Florence, Genoa and Venice were making good money from wool weaving. The Spanish, jealously guarding their flocks of wool-rich merinos (see page 125), were able to fund foreign explorations including that of Columbus with profits from the wool trade.

In the Middle Ages European monasteries grew rich on the profits of the wool trade. The Cistercian monks were so confident of their profits that they would forward-sell their wool. However, when a disastrous outbreak of sheep scab killed thousands of flocks it triggered a devastating credit crunch and temporarily destroyed confidence in the European wool trade.

When in the 16th century the English King Henry VIII sacked his monasteries and stole their sheep (see page 49), he founded a wool trade that, by the 17th century, accounted for two-thirds of all British exports. Britain's 19th-century Industrial Revolution was powered by the mechanisation of the wool industry, which had until then been a staple of the cottage economy. The British, like the Spanish, attempted to prevent other nations, the United States in particular, from profiting from wool.

There were, however, alternatives: cotton from the Americas, for example, and silk from the Far East. Then there was the South American llama (with its entrancing Latin title *Lama glama*). Like the sheep, the llama was eaten for its meat. It was also a sturdy pack animal, and even as dependable a guard as the dog. The llama also produced a weaveable coat that, although technically not a wool, nevertheless served to keep its owners warm in the field.

Yet sheep dutifully produced a fresh fleece every year on land that would not otherwise have turned a profit. Among the estimated one billion sheep in the world there are dozens of different breeds, but most can be divided into 'longwools' such as the French Rambouillet and the Lincolnshire longwools; 'shortwools', regarded as a better provider of meat than wool; and hardy hill breeds such as the Cumbrian herdwick, good for meat and wool – one of the herdwick's more famous breeders was the children's author, Beatrix Potter.

Hand weaving was an arduous process: the fleece was sheared in one piece, 'carded' to straighten the wool fibres and separate them from the fleece – a process often involving the fieldside teasel plant – and then spun on the spinning wheel to produce lengths of yarn. The yarn was wound on to a reel or 'weasel' – the popping sound of the full reel celebrated in the traditional nursery rhyme 'pop goes the weasel' – when it was ready for dyeing and weaving.

In time, local knitters and weavers became renowned for the products of their labours – for example, the famous sweaters from the Aran Isles off the coast of Ireland. Their stitching developed a vocabulary of its own: the trellis stitch mirrored the pattern of the stonewalled fields; the cable stitch their fishing ropes; and the diamond stitch their nets. The blackberry stitch, a pattern of three points, represented the Holy Trinity; and the double zigzag, the ups and downs

'The sheep is frightened at everything.'

William Cobbett, *Cottage Economy*, 1822

of married life. It is said that so distinctive was each stitch that the home of an unknown drowned sailor could be established from the stitch of his sweater.

But it wasn't just woolenwear that was distinctive in character. Smugglers moving over the Spanish border into Portugal in the 1780s drove a curious cargo before them: a small flock of sheep. The sheep were merinos destined for the court of King George III of England, nicknamed 'Farmer George' for his passion for agricultural affairs. The merino, assured the King's advisor Sir Joseph Banks – who was reputedly behind the smuggling – would thrive in the new country and bring in the kind of revenues then being enjoyed by the King of Spain, from whom, in theory, the flock had been smuggled.

The merino – which originated in Spain, or in North Africa – was remarkable. Small and bright-eyed, it could subsist on poor grazing and, thanks to its fleece of the finest, softest wool, survive extremes of cold. The merino's wool was so fine it could be woven into billiard-table cloth, and so dense it was judged three times better than that of most other breeds. The Spanish King's Castilian empire had grown up on the woolly backs of the merinos and a lucrative trade with Flanders. Not that the animals spent much time in a field: instead they were relentlessly driven along their migration routes, the *cañadas*, following the seasonal pastures as they crossed the Meseta, the vast central tableland of Spain. So vital were the merinos to Spain's economy that the Spanish sheep breeders' association, the Mesta, outlawed their export. Hence King George's subterfuge.

But the smuggled herd failed to impress the King who sent a request for better breeding stock direct to Spain. The Spanish King obliged – he also sent sheep to Germany, France and, in 1789, South Africa – but the breed failed to flourish as well as British breeds such as the Shetland, which produced a wool almost as fine as the merino's.

The Spanish flock was kept at Kew near London until they were sold off in 1803. The merinos, however, were to do very well in the British colony of Australia. In the 1950s Australians were shepherding around 131 million sheep, mostly merinos – 15 per cent of the world's total – and producing almost 30 per cent of the world's wool. And it all began with a British plan to relieve overcrowding in its prisons. Between 1788 and 1850 more than 160,000 convicts were sent to the penal colonies of New South Wales, Australia. The First Fleet bearing

Merino sheep were introduced to Australia in the 18th century along with boatloads of British convicts. In spite of early struggles they have gone on to flourish.

the first convicts reached Port Jackson on 26 January, 1788 – the date is commemorated as Australia Day – together with a flock of Cape-bred sheep collected en route from South Africa. The sheep, like the settlers, languished in the savage and arid conditions. In 1791 a supply ship brought in extra sheep, but by November that year there were only one ram, 50 ewes and six lambs left on the whole continent.

By 1792, although most of the remaining sheep had been eaten, a few breeders had started flocks. There was even one surviving ewe from the First Fleet in the flock of Edward Elliott of Ponds, Parramatta. Then in 1796 a Captain Water-house imported Australia's first Spanish merinos from the flock of the late Dutch commandant on the Cape of Good Hope – the commandant had imported his merinos from his home in the Netherlands.

Most of the settlers were more interested in mutton than wool, and Water-house struggled to sell them. However, one of his buyers, John Macarthur, bought and bred the merinos along with other breeds including some Irish sheep, Southdowns and Teeswaters. A sample of the fleeces sent to Britain caught the attention of the British wool buyers who were impressed by their quality. Macarthur eventually left Australia, but for now he was persuaded to stay, having been granted 2,800 hectares (7,000 acres) of land and provided with some stud animals from the original royal flock of merinos at Kew.

In 1813 new grazing lands in the west were opened up when settlers crossed the Blue Mountains. By now the miserable one ram, 50 ewes and six lambs had increased to 65,000 sheep based on Spanish merinos. There were another 19,000 in Tasmania. Diseases such as scab and footrot continued to plague sheep flocks on the coastal plains, but the country's inland pastures proved perfect for what was to become Australia's thriving sheep industry.

Hogs and Swine

Characterised as a slovenly, gluttonous and dirty creature, the pig receives a poor press. To 'drive one's pigs to market' is to snore; to buy a 'pig in a poke' is to make a foolish purchase – possibly of the runt, or 'St. Anthony's pig'; and to 'pig it' is to eat greedily. Yet, according to the testimony of the swineherd, the pig is fastidiously clean, highly sensitive and arguably our oldest animal ally after the dog. The pig has proven a generous creature too; after all, as the idiom has it, the only part of a pig for which there is no use is its squeal.

The modern pig was bred by crossing hogs from Southeast Asia with European pigs: the famous Tamworth probably owes its russet tones to the red jungle pigs of India. The pig could be bred to be clever, if finding the rare truffle without snuffling it down is a mark of cleverness. It could be bred for bulk: the 'large whites', also known as Yorkshires, were grown to tremendous sizes. One, illustrated by a field artist in 1809, weighed 609.6 kilograms (1,344 pounds), and measured 3 metres (9 feet 10 inches) long. The three-year-old pig was put on exhibition in England and earned £3,000 in ticket sales.

The pig is happiest in the wild forest – English swineherds enjoyed the rights of *pannage*, allowing them to feed their animals on the forests' fallen acorns and beech mast. But the widespread loss of forests was followed by intense breeding programs, which saw the pig transformed into a meat machine. Advanced methods of pig keeping and breeding coincided with the Western world's 19th-century exodus from country to town. A big beneficiary in England was the Berkshire, a hog fed on the by-products of London's bakeries, breweries, cheese makers and distilleries. The Berkshire and its crossbreeds would eventually be exported to Europe, Asia and North America, and it was the Berkshire that developed into the distinctive lop-eared, white landrace of Sweden, Norway, Germany, Finland, the Netherlands, Belgium, America and above all Denmark.

Curiously too it was the Berkshire that the English novelist George Orwell chose to personify as Napoleon, one of a pair of bullying dictators in his satirical novel on the follies of human civilisation, *Animal Farm*. Another world-famous literary Berkshire was Empress, bred by Clarence, ninth Earl of Emsworth. According to her real creator, novelist P. G. Wodehouse, Empress was the Earl's preferred companion and the winner of the silver medal at the Shropshire Agricultural Show's Fat Pig event thanks to her size and her schoolgirl's complexion.

Goats

Given the opportunity, it is said that the goat would eat its way around the world. In Burma the goat was blamed for any eclipse: it was said to have eaten the sun or the moon. Foraging by goats has already decimated the grazing in many countries, yet the goat's predilection for thorny fodder has earned it some friends: in southeast America where abandoned farm pastures were invaded by the old homesteaders' roses and vines, it is goats, rather than herbicides, that have been employed to clear the fields of these invasive foreigners. On the grassy balds – mountain summits or crests covered with vegetation – of the sub-alpine meadows in the southern Appalachians, goats have been carrying out a managed defoliation of the invasive Canadian blackberry, not only helping preserve the pastureland, but also creating open spaces for the return of the rare Gray's lily.

Every nation is proud of its particular breed: the golden Guernsey from the Channel Island of the same name – although its bloodlines were traceable back to the wild goats of Syria and Malta; the pygmy goats of North Africa; and the Saanen and Saanen Toggenburg, from the valleys of the Swiss canton of Berne.

The wild mountain goat (*Capra aegagus*) provided the parentage for the first domestic goats that trotted out of the Fertile Crescent 10,000 years ago. Since then different breeds developed different traits: European breeds were renowned for their milk, fine cheese, yoghurt and even chocolate; eastern or Nubian goats for their meat and milk; and breeds such as the mohair-producing Angoras from Ankara, Turkey, and the cashmere from Kashmir for their fine wool.

The goat has proven to be a great provider. The meat was good, the milk, which was easier to digest than cow's milk, was plentiful. Parchment made from goat hide was regarded as the best that money could buy. Their fat provided good tallow for candles and, once cashmere fabrics began making their way westward out of Tibet, the undercoat was considered superior to the finest sheep wool.

And yet there was something about the goat. The 18th-century livestock improvers turned their nose up at advancing goat breeds – they left deer alone too – either because they regarded it as the poor man's cow or because they held an age-old conviction that the beast was inherently evil. Expressions such as 'separating the sheep from the goats' (dividing the trustworthy from the untrustworthy), 'getting one's goat' (making one annoyed), or 'being turned into a scapegoat' (a biblical reference to the sins heaped upon Azazel's goat before it was sent out into the wilderness) seem to confirm the prejudice.

Poultry

Come dawn the cockerel will throw back his head and let out what Shakespeare called the 'trumpet of the morn'. Up and down the village the other cocks, which had doubtless intended to be first, reply: 'cock-a-doodle-do'. In Wales the crowing of a white cock was considered lucky, unless it crowed around midnight, when it presaged a death. The cockerel's crow is even said to make the Devil take flight. And it's said that windvanes in the form of cockerels were placed on many church spires as a reminder, in the Christian tale, of Peter's denial of Christ, which had been accompanied by the crowing of a cockerel.

In all probability poultry keeping started not with egg production, but cock fighting. The sport was popular in the Middle East and the Orient and game birds such as the *aseel* or *asil*, one of the original Indian birds, were bred for the cock pit. Fighting birds included the Madras aseel and Rajah aseel, the Indian game or Cornish, the Japanese Shamo (in Japanese, *Shamo* simply means fighter) and the Asiatic Malay.

The domestic chickens probably evolved from the common or red jungle fowl. By the year 3200 B.C.E. backyard hens were being kept in Asia, particularly in India. Those ancient keepers would be dismayed to see how their progeny fare today, entrapped in factory buildings. 'Cramming', wrote William Cobbett, 'is a nasty thing, and quite unnecessary.' The modern hen lays twice the number of eggs that she did 80 years ago, but mostly while incarcerated in factory farms. Some countries, Sweden and Switzerland among them, have legislated against cage- or battery-hen systems.

Birds fare better in the field. 'My birds are allowed the run of the field and seem to thrive exceedingly well', wrote one proud smallholder in an 1890s country magazine. She was writing at a time of change in the poultry world. There are more chickens than any other bird in the world, and an estimated third live alongside their host families, laying where they can and avoiding the hatchet when there is a shortage of meat for the pot. However, in 1852 the British Queen Victoria expressed her 'amusement' at the gift of nine Brahmas from India. This royal approval sparked a general interest in cultivating and improving the different hen breeds. There was the stout, black Orpington and the Sussex, both from southeast England. There were ill-tempered Malays, tall, rangy birds bred for the cock pit, and Dorkings, a bird curiously equipped with an extra toe. One of the favourite smallholder breeds was the Rhode Island red, a bird from the state of Rhode Island in America. While some hens were more fit for a life of laying, and others better suited to the pot, the Rhode Island red was considered a good all-rounder.

'Cramming is a nasty thing, and quite unnecessary.'

William Cobbett, *Cottage Economy*, 1822

Ducks, geese, turkeys and guinea fowl are almost as important to the field economy as the chicken. Their feathers once provided writing quills, stuffing for the best mattresses and pillows, and arrow flights. And when it was time to drive the geese to market, the gooseherd dipped their feet in tar to protect them from the road stone. However, the cackling goose provided an additional service, that of 'watchgoose', for when a goose is alarmed it likes to make itself heard: legend has it that it was a flock of geese that alerted Rome's slumbering sentinels when the city came under siege in 390 B.C.E.

Turkeys, too, were shod for the drive to market, but when it comes to turkeys there is no wilder sight than a flock of feral turkeys bustling down an African road, wings akimbo. Yet they were not native to Africa. For the turkey is yet another American import, domesticated by the Aztecs for its meat and feathers. By the time the Spanish conquistadores arrived in the Americas, turkey was the staple meat of the Aztecs, Mayans and Incas, and it was the conquistadores who introduced the turkey to Europe. Why then was the bird named after a country on the Anatolian peninsula? Quite simply, Europeans, who mistook the turkey for a guinea fowl, named it after the place from which they thought, misguidedly, it had originated.

Wild at Heart

At dawn and dusk when the workers have tramped home to their suppers, the field comes alive. A shy group of deer emerges to graze at the margins; an otter risks crossing from one brook to another. Wild goats come down from the hills to browse as foxes and badgers roam free. This is the time for the hedgehog and rabbit, the stoat and weasel, the bear and the moose to wander at liberty. Caution is still called for, though: many of these animals have been hunted for both sport and for the pot.

Meanwhile humans battle to cut crop losses to wildlife. Some estimates put the loss of food to wildlife, both in the field and in storage, as high as a third; in parts of Latin America it could be as high as 40 per cent.

Rodents represent over 40 per cent of all mammals, and although only a few of the 1,700 species are genuine pests – the southern grasshopper mouse is happy scavenging scorpions and ants, for example – rats are believed to eat 40 million metric tons of human food every year. But there are also other pestilential creatures in the field, none more so than the rabbit.

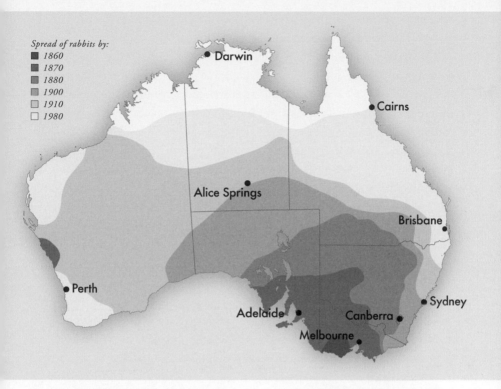

The spread of rabbits throughout Australia has been extremely rapid. Released in Christmas 1859 near Melbourne, the plague reached Adelaide within 10 years, Sydney and Alice Springs within 40 years, and Cairns and Perth in just over a hundred years.

The European rabbit started out in the arid north and west of Africa and Iberia before being introduced to the rest of Europe. Rabbits graze: eight bunnies can munch their way through as much grass as a sheep, and the first record of rabbit damage in Britain was in 1340 when they ate the Bishop of Chichester's wheat. At the beginning of the 19th century rabbits were introduced to Australia and, a century ago, to Argentina, from where they spread into Chile.

The history of the introduction of non-indigenous animals is a salutary one, milestoned by mistakes. When the mongoose and cat were introduced to control rats in the Caribbean and many Indian Ocean and Pacific islands, they eradicated much of the native wildlife. Possums were taken to New Zealand in 1837 to be farmed for their fur. They went wild and continue to decimate native trees on which wildlife feed, and to eat the eggs of native birds. Elsewhere, hedgehogs let loose in the Outer Hebrides in 1974 to tackle the problem of garden slugs preyed instead on the eggs of ground-nesting wild birds.

The same story is true of the rabbit. In the early 1950s France was reporting dramatic crop losses to rabbits. In Australia and New Zealand the situation was even worse, with some New Zealanders abandoning farming to hunt rabbits for their fur, while Australians tried to string long rabbit-proof fences across their country to contain the problem. These, however, failed to finish off the rabbit.

The solution was myxomatosis, a virus first found in the South American forests by Brazilian scientists in 1879. In 1950 myxomatosis was released in the Murray Valley, Australia, carried by mosquitoes, in France it was introduced in 1952, and in Britain in 1953. The spectacle of rabbits dying everywhere distressed many people, but myxomatosis did temporarily halt the plague of rabbits. Yet now the animals, having developed a degree of immunity to the disease, are once again on the increase. In Australia, despite these efforts to control it, the rabbit remains one of the most abundant animals on the continent.

In most instances, however, wildlife is losing out to the field. In many parts of the developed world more wildlife can be found in urban areas than in an arable field of the same size, because of its lack of variety. In non-mechanised farming communities wildlife is tolerated as long as it behaves.

Hunting animals can damage wild stocks, but the loss of ancient agricultural systems, of permanent pastures, hedges and wetland meadows that are replaced by intensively farmed fields causes more harm to wildlife communities than hunting. Conservation efforts go some way to redressing the balance. They include the captive breeding of wild creatures that are then released into the wild – as happened with the California condor in the 1980s, the white rhino in South Africa and the red kite in Wales and England – wildlife tourism and international agreements on the movements of live wild animals; and killing for conservation, which is rarely a popular solution. In the Outer Hebrides plans to cull the hedgehog were met with vigorous campaigns to save it. Although they represent little more than 1 per cent of the area of most countries, national parks also help to protect wildlife. But above all, the most effective conservation method is habitat protection. Fields with wide, unsprayed headlands, a corner copse of trees, or a restored pond work wonders for wildlife.

While we have already covered some of the relatively few mammals that have been domesticated, it is now time to turn our attention to those that remain wild. Those that might be found in the field range from mice and bats so small they could fit in the palm of the hand, to the lumbering African elephant.

Mammals evolved as small rat-like creatures from their mammal-like reptilian ancestors 200 million years ago and started to diversify around 50 million years ago: horses, camels, elephants, monkeys and rodents developed in the Northern Hemisphere with predatory wolves, bears and cats close on their heels. South America, the southeast of the United States and Australia became home to the marsupials, which carry their young in a pouch, such as the Virginian opossum, the kangaroo and the koala – of the 334 species of marsupials, over 200 are indigenous to Australia.

Some mammals have adapted to the field better than others. For example, the brown rat (*Rattus norvegicus*), also known as the common or Norwegian rat, is one of the most successful mammals on the planet. Where there are no people, there are rarely any rats. The rat, one of the largest of the 56 species of *Rattus*, may have originated in China, spreading into Europe more gradually than its close cousin, the ship or black rat (*Rattus rattus*). The brown rat is capable of breeding a cataclysm of rats: one pair could theoretically produce 15,000 animals in a year, but the creature keeps a close control on its fertility in a way that its hosts, people, do not. However, with one eye on the granary, and the other on a safe and warm place to raise its young, the rat has always been on an inevitable collision course with the farmer. Aside from regular rat hunts when the farmhands took their terriers to the barn to flush out the rodents, the farmer played on one of the rat's weaknesses: its inability to vomit. Once poisoned, the rat is doomed, although the others in the colony will learn rapidly from its mistake and avoid the poisoned bait. In the 1950s warfarin was introduced, a poison that was undetectable in bait and, after a delay long enough to confuse the other rats, caused fatal internal bleeding. In spite of such measures, half a century later the rat is anything but down and out.

It's a similar story for other grassland mammals such as the mole, shrew, stoat, hare and rabbit, or other mammals that benefit from the field. If, however, there was one mammal that should never have been allowed to stray beyond its home territory it would have to be the rabbit.

On the Wing

At dusk over a lake in Andalusia, Spain, the evening air is filled suddenly with mournful cries. A flock of bee-eaters descends for their final feed of the day. Elsewhere, flocks of black-headed gulls gather behind a plough to feed on the worms that have been exposed by the ploughshare. White storks, those harbingers of good fortune, step gingerly through a field of cut hay in Eastern Europe, spearing any small creatures they find. Barn owls set out at dusk to quarter the field on silent wings. Rooks, ravens and magpies squabble loudly over carrion.

Birds are the most conspicuous creatures of many fields, and their diversity is extraordinary. The high cries that echo over the fields of winter wheat in Western Europe are the calls of the over-wintering fieldfare. In the mountainous areas of Africa the scarlet-tufted malachite sunbird with its long, narrow plumes, hops from branch to branch. The hoopoe zigzags through an olive grove, lifting its mad head crest as it lands to lift a lizard – Arabs once believed that the hoopoe's curious walk signified the presence of water underground. On the dry coastal areas of Southeast Asia the repetitive cheeping of the savannah nightjar sounds monotonously for half an hour at dusk and dawn. In French forest groves nightingales call in the night. In legend the nightingale was said to fear snakes and, in order to stay awake and alert all night, impaled its breast upon a thorn: his mournful night song reflects his pain.

'The merl, the mavys, and the nichtyngale, With merry notes mirthfully furth brest', wrote the 16th-century Bishop of Dunkeld, Gavin Douglas, of the hawk, the song thrush and the nightingale in his translation of Virgil's *Aeneid*.

The children, charged with scaring the birds away as the field was sown, chanted a different verse: 'Away birds, away, Take a little, and leave a little, And do not come again; For if you do, I will shoot you through, And there is an end to you.' Seed-sowing time – heralded in America by the first of the bobolinks and orioles – was feeding time for many birds. 'One for the cut worm, One for the crow; One for the blackbird, And three to grow.'

Yet birds provide a service that is not always appreciated by the field worker: kites, harriers and hawks help keep down rodent populations; the red-headed woodpeckers of North America will hawk insects in flight, while their European cousin, the green woodpecker, methodically eats trails of ants. But there can be no closer relationship between people and wild birds than in the sky burials of

'The merl, the mavys, and the nichtyngale,
With merry noties mirthfully furth brest.'

Gavin Douglas, *Eneados*, 16th century

Tibet and northern India where the dead are taken into the fields so they can be cleaned away by the local vultures, ravens and hawks.

The contribution of birds to the field cannot be measured in purely economic terms. Where would we be without the 'bird that cuts the airy way, In an immense world of delight', as William Blake wrote in his *Marriage of Heaven and Hell* (1790)? The skies of northern Europe would be much impoverished without the lapwing, foraging in ploughed fields from Scandinavia to the Mediterranean. And life on the land would never be the same without the hummingbird and the eagle, the wheatear – the French call it the *culblanc,* for here wheat means 'whit' or 'white', and 'ears' translates as the vulgar 'arse' – or the skylark, celebrated by the composer Ralph Vaughan Williams' 'Lark Ascending', a piece of music with the power to make grown men cry.

Reptiles and Amphibians

More closely related to birds than mammals, these secretive creatures made the move from an aquatic lifestyle to the damp margins of the land around 350 million years ago, long before the first field was established. Yet their survival in the field is often precarious. Most move slowly, occupy a limited range – in some cases just a few human paces – and are especially sensitive to habitat change.

The loss of a pond, or the removal of traditional drainage ditches, can kill whole colonies. Reptiles and amphibians are vulnerable to pesticides and pollution and the decline or disappearance of any species acts as a warning sign that all is not well in the field. The World Conservation Union estimates that more than 2,150 species, including a third of the world's frogs, are endangered. Being 'cold-blooded' they can live for days, even months, without food, but they need external sources of heat to survive. In colder climates they must bask by day and hibernate during the winter. Conversely, in warmer climes they rest up in the heat of the day and hunt for food only at night.

Some have a long lifespan: toads have been known to live for over 30 years, while one Japanese giant salamander survived in captivity for 55 years. One American box turtle showed its age in a curious way: found in Hope Valley in the northeastern United States, the turtle was carrying a piece of graffiti on its back: a date, 1844, and the initials of a mischievous farm boy, carved on its carapace. Tracing the history of the farming family back proved 'Old 1844', as he became known, to be 138 years old.

There are over 5,000 different species of amphibians – newts, salamanders, frogs and toads – although many species are thought to be becoming extinct even before they have been found and named. Amphibians (from the Greek *amphi* and *bios*, 'two lives', a reference to their passing part of their lives in water and part on land) are concentrated in the Northern Hemisphere, in Europe and North, Central and South America. The most widespread, the frogs and toads, are found in fields everywhere apart from Antarctica.

The reptiles – snakes, lizards, turtles, tortoises, crocodiles and alligators – are more prevalent in the tropical regions: Central and South America, West and Central Africa and Southeast Asia. Some are more visible than others: the boa, which can grow to over 3 metres (10 feet) and is capable of consuming a careless dog, performs the useful service of disposing of the local rat population, but snakes are nevertheless relentlessly persecuted – a problem that the American western hognose snake tries to get around by feigning death when cornered. In the early days of the American settlers, rattlesnake round-ups were organised as a means of reducing the snake population around local farms, but by the 20th century the round-ups had degenerated into routine and unnecessary slaughter. Yet the western diamond rattlesnakes, which are regularly run over by motorists, still make a significant impact on rodent and rabbit numbers. The puff adder vies with the black mamba for first place as Africa's most deadly snake, and both are persecuted as a consequence.

There are occasional success stories, however. The alligator, which earned its name from America's Spanish settlers who mistook it for a lizard, *el lagarto*, and which was facing extinction in Florida, has made a comeback in some places thanks to conservation areas and a hunting ban. The Chinese alligator, however, has suffered badly from the loss of habitat to rice paddy fields. Now the alligator has even become a farm animal, prized for its meat and hide, just as crocodile farming has taken off in places such as Southeast Asia and parts of southern Africa.

Insects: Friend or Foe?

Wanted posters started appearing outside British police stations in the 1950s seeking information, not on some escaped felon, but on an attractive little black-and-yellow beetle, the Colorado. Having escaped from its confines in the Rocky Mountains of America, the Colorado beetle made its way by ship or plane across the Atlantic into Europe and was now wreaking havoc in the fields.

HEATHER

Name: Common heather
(*Calluna vulgaris*)

What it's like: The shrubby, low-growing perennial plant that grows on the acidic soils of Europe's heaths and moors earns its name from its one-time use as a brush. *Calluna* comes from the Greek for 'to sweep'. Also known as ling, heather was used to thatch the roofs of highland cottages and as a fragrant bedding for their occupants.

Grazed by sheep, and by deer in winter when the animals can crop the tops of the plants through the snow, heather provides natural shelter for wild grouse.

A sprig of white-flowering heather is regarded as a lucky charm and the spectacular flowering of heather in late summer is celebrated in the old music hall song of Harry Lauder (1870–1950): 'I loved a lassie, a bonnie, bonnie lassie; She's as sweet as the heather, the bonnie, bloomin' heather.'

The blooming of the heather triggers a buzz of bees, and heather-flavoured honey is highly prized for its taste and thick texture. Bee keepers will purposely station their hives amongst the heather for this purpose. Brewers in the Scottish Highlands still harvest the flowering tips of the plant for the manufacture of a fragrant heather ale.

Where it's grown: From Europe across to Asia. It has been introduced to other countries, including the United States, by Scottish settlers. Its introduction has caused problems in countries like New Zealand where it is now classed as an invasive weed, and is a particular threat in the national parks.

Insects are both foe and friend in the field. The orchard could not survive without insects. Yet around 50 per cent of the world's cotton would be lost if predatory insects were allowed to roam free.

There are an estimated 20 to 30 million insects in the world. Most have yet to be named and many are still being discovered. They range from grasshoppers and cockroaches, to bees, butterflies and wasps. Annoying as they are at the picnic table, wasps take crop insects to feed their grubs and, like the honey bee, many pollinate crops. But the red-rust flour beetle feeds, as its name suggests, on ground grain, the grain weevil makes its home inside grain kernels, and a plague of locusts can strip a field in a matter of hours.

Sometimes it is the fields themselves that are the root cause of the problem. Enter the Colorado beetle. The Colorado was not a problem as long as it fed on the wild sand-bur of the Rocky Mountains, but when in the 1850s miners began planting their potato fields the beetle ravaged the crop and spread, at the rate of 110 kilometres (70 miles) a year, towards the Atlantic. Today in Europe, only the UK, Republic of Ireland, Balearic Islands, Cyprus, Malta, Sweden and Finland are free of the Colorado beetle.

It was a similar story with the parasite that causes the fatal sleeping sickness. The parasite caused little problem to its hosts, the wild animals of central Africa. Seeking to improve on the indigenous cattle such as the Brahman, European breeds such as Herefords, Aberdeen Angus, Murray greys and Frieslands were introduced. Transmitted by flies, the parasite attacked the new breeds and promptly became a problem. The Zulu called the disease *nagana*, meaning the cattle were 'depressed'.

Farmers fought back with various inorganic, organic and natural poisons, each in their own way dangerous to humans. The first, inorganic poisons, which included substances such as sulphur – used as a fumigant since biblical times – and arsenic in the form of copper arsenite, used to control bugs such as the Colorado beetle, eventually proved too hazardous because they also contaminated the soil. Next came the organochlorides including the notorious DDT (Dichlorodiphenyltrichloroethane). But these poisons built up in the fatty tissues of animals that preyed on the insects. This process, known as bioaccumulation, saw top predators such as birds of prey seriously affected, while traces of organochlorides were even found in animals and birds in Antarctica.

Beehives in a Californian cherry orchard are an integral part of the field's ecosystem. Hives are sometimes transported great distances to pollinate crops.

It was time to turn to the organophosphates. These, the dominant pesticides of the 21st century, are related to nerve gases developed in World War II and, although more toxic than the organochlorides, were designed to be shorter-lived and so less persistent in the environment. Although organophosphates degrade faster than the organochlorides, they have greater acute toxicity, posing risks to people who may be exposed to large amounts.

There were also systemic organophosphates, which could be carried up in the sap of the growing plants, and synthetic pyrethroids, based on the naturally occurring insecticides produced by the pyrethrum plant, as well as less effective chemicals such as nicotine from the tobacco plant.

Mistakes made over the use of organochlorides, and the impact of pesticides generally on insects beneficial to life in the field, led to new research into an old method: biological control. One early example concerned the cottony cushion scale insect, accidentally imported from Australia, that had been devastating Californian orange groves in the late 19th century. This pest was brought under control by the introduction of an Australian ladybug. Nevertheless there are concerns that biological controls could cause further imbalances.

The honey bee – of which there are a number of species and subspecies – is the field's best friend. Without this insect's pollinating powers an estimated 80 per cent of the world's crops, or a third of the food we eat, would not grow. In North America bees are transported thousands of miles on trucks to pollinate crops ranging from apples, almonds, peaches and soya beans to cherries, melons and strawberries.

The honey bee has long been recognised for its contribution to agriculture, and bee legends are accordingly universal. The god Zeus turned the nymph Melissa into a bee and rewarded her with the ability to propagate her kind without recourse to a male. In fact the average bee hive consists of 50,000 workers, 1,000 drones and one queen bee, who, once she has mated with several drones, devotes the rest of her life to laying eggs. In Hindu mythology Vishnu is represented as a blue bee on a lotus flower, while Kama, the god of love, bears a bow with a string made from a chain of bees. One tale from the Ukraine tells of St. Sossima bringing bees from Egypt in a hollowed-out reed. The Ethiopian town of Lalibela – literally 'the bee recognises the king' – was named after its 12th-century King Lalibela, whose mother was said to have realised his royal virtues when she spotted a swarm of bees by his cradle.

The superstitions surrounding the welfare of bees are equally numerous. In Europe, if the hive was not formally told of the death of their owner, the bees would die. Planting lemon balm around a hive was said to keep bees from abandoning the hive in a swarm, and the plant was also rubbed around the inside of a new hive to help the bees settle in – its Latin name *Melissa officinalis* reflects the link, *melissa* being Greek for a honey bee. Similarly, beating metal pots was reputed to calm a swarm down and help them enter a new hive.

To create a swarm of bees and a dependable source of honey, according to Virgil, the bee keeper should butcher a beast and place tree boughs, thyme and rosemary beneath the body.

'How does the little busy bee, Improve each shining hour, And gather honey all the day, From every opening flower?' wondered Isaac Watts in *Against Idleness and Mischief*. Bees transform flower nectars, watery sugar solutions, into honey in the hive. The colours vary with the flower crop: honey from rosebay willow herb is pale, white clover creates a light honey, tree blossom a dark honey. Aromatic plants flavour the honey: sage, lavender and marjoram, or the famous rosemary honeys of Narbonne, France, and pine honey from Germany. Mead was made from honey, while the beeswax could be turned into the best candles, used to seal jars, and to make wax casts of the living – or dead: Madame Marie Tussaud made beeswax death masks of Louis XVI and Marie Antoinette after their beheading during the French Revolution.

But in the early 21st century something started to go wrong with the honey bees. Hives of bees have been known to die suddenly since the late 19th century, suffering from spring dwindle or May disease. But the incidences of what has become known as Colony Collapse Disorder (CCD) have rocketed since it was first reported in North America in 2006. Colony collapses have spread through hives in the United States, Canada, Italy, France, Belgium, Germany, Britain and the Mediterranean countries with reported losses of 30 per cent, even 50 per cent in parts of Italy. Possible causes include loss of habitat, pesticides, genetically modified crops, global warming, drought and radiation from mobile phone masts. But at the time of writing scientists have yet to find a definitive explanation, and a method of prevention or cure remains elusive.

Chapter Six

TOOLS AND
TECHNOLOGY

As fields have developed, so has the technology used to tend them. Starting with the plough – which predates the wheel as an invention – a whole range of equipment has evolved to fit every conceivable function, culminating in the heavy machinery of today's industrial agriculture. Here the most interesting of these devices, their usage and the people who invented them are explored.

Hand Tools

In medieval times the fields of France, Germany, Scandinavia, the Low Countries and England were ripe for cultivation. Compared to the east and south of Europe, the climate in the north and west was more temperate, the rainfall more reliable and the plains as broad and potentially fertile as those that would stretch out before the new American settlers half a millennium later. Farming methods were improving. New crops such as beans and peas were adding nitrogen to the soil and the first farming manuals were being painstakingly inscribed on monastic parchment.

Thomas Malthus in his *Essay on the Principle of Population*, published in 1798, proposed that in order for any population to sustain growth it was necessary to 'turn up fresh soil, and to manure and improve more completely what was already in tillage; till ultimately the means of subsistence becomes in the same proportion to the population.' The population of Europe seemed to bear out his thesis, for it grew with the spread of the field. The population had risen from an estimated 40 million in 1000 c.e. to more than 70 million three centuries later, before the Black Death scythed its way through Europe killing about a third of its population.

The field owners of northern Europe, meanwhile, were considerably better off than those who worked them. The lords of the land had problems to contend with. They had to deal with primitive banking arrangements since the medieval Italians were only just beginning to found the business of banking. They had to

A medieval peasant ploughs the field and the population of medieval Europe rises on the back of his labours. Agricultural output increased, but life was hard for peasants.

risk capital on insecure loans like harvest credit and cope with the vagaries of the weather – the poor harvests of the 1320s may well have paved the way for the Black Death. But the lord fared better than his subjects.

The serfs who laboured with their hand tools in their masters' fields did so on a diet of around 2,000 calories a day. This was the best they could hope to extract from their diet of grits and thin gruels, the little that was left after they had surrendered three-quarters of the produce of their labours to the landlord in tithes, 'customs' and taxes. However, as fields were founded and farmed across Europe, and as the population rose, some managed to break free from serfdom and find payment instead of servitude for their labour. The first to walk free were the tool makers.

A man who could fashion a good ash bow for the ox yoke was as indispensable as the man who could manage six oxen in a line. The family with a reputation for stitching strong donkey collars that increased the beast's pulling power without chafing away at the animal's flesh was as valuable as the rushworkers and their bee skeps, buckets and poultry nesting boxes. A good tool made work easier and cut labour costs.

Among the world's wealthy nations craftwork has become an absorbing and pleasing pastime, but in the subsistence economy, then and now, craft workers have shown extraordinary ingenuity in their ability to transform raw materials into tools for the field: ladder-backed farm chairs and hand-stitched cold-weather jackets; wooden egg racks and wicker donkey panniers; bramble baskets and timber turnip slicers; burden ropes, straw saddles, and even toys fashioned from discarded tin cans. Foremost among the craftspeople were the ironmasters (see page 151) but the hedge carpenter, the sawyer, stone mason, cooper, weaver and spinner, the thatcher, the well digger, basket maker and rope maker all contributed to the local economy. And it was indeed a local business. The eel traps and dog muzzles of a willow worker in the Hook of Holland developed along distinctively different lines from the eel traps of a willow weaver on England's Somerset Levels or the sally saucers – or wicker potato trays – and herring crans of a weaver working the willow beds of Lough Neagh in Ireland.

Nowhere is this individuality more pronounced than in the dairy with its butter stamps and pats, butter scales and milk separators, box churns that stood on the plank-top table of the farmhouse, or great barrel butter churns that had to be turned for hours in cold weather. The Irish playwright John Millington Synge was entranced by the handcrafts of the remote Aran islanders – he had stayed on the islands, off the west coast of Ireland, and later wrote about his visit in *The Aran Islands* (1907). 'Every article on these islands has an almost personal

'As I had little aid from horses or cattle, or hired men or boys, or improved implements of husbandry, I was much slower, and became much more intimate with my beans than usual.'

Henry David Thoreau, *Walden and Other Writings*, 1854

character which gives this simple life, where all art is unknown, something of the artistic beauty of medieval life.'

Another country commentator, Henry David Thoreau, decided that sticking to his hand tools, especially his hoe, brought him closer to the business of field work: 'As I had little aid from horses or cattle, or hired men or boys, or improved implements of husbandry, I was much slower, and became much more intimate with my beans than usual.'

Spade and Hoe

Seeds liberally scattered across a bare field will feed the birds before they will grow. Instead the soil must be turned, broken up and ground down into a fine *tilth* and the seeds buried within it.

One way to cultivate the field was with that forerunner of the spade, the mattock or, in Ireland, the *matóg*. The mattock was spade, hoe, trencher and root digger in one. With its broad blade at one end and blunt point at the other, it was a close relative of the adze, the house builder's axe used to fashion boughs of green and unseasoned oak into house beams, and the butcher's poleaxe used to dispatch an animal with a single blow to the brow. The mattock was gradually replaced by the pronged fork, the hoe and the spade as metal technology improved, but while it was pushed to the back of the barn in the West, it can still be seen carving up the field in some countries.

In the Irish Catholic calendar, 1 September is the feast day of the patron saint of gardening and the spade, St. Fiacre. He is said to have earned his saint-hood when in the seventh century he left his native Ireland for France. Here, near what is now Saint-Fiacre-en-Brie in France, Bishop Faro of Meaux presented Fiacre with a piece of land to found a monastery. The size of the monastery, Faro told Fiacre, depended on how much of a field the priest could dig in a day. Fiacre took up his trusty spade at dawn and by sunset had turned the sod of no less than 9 acres (3.6 hectares). Fiacre's hermitage was founded on the site – it is famed for its powers to cure haemorrhoids – and at Meaux a chapel and shrine were dedicated to the good man and his spade. He would also be remembered by Parisian drivers of the four-wheeled cab, or *fiacre*, which first appeared for hire close by the Hôtel Saint-Fiacre.

Irish links with the field spade continued down the ages. Gangs of Irish inland navigators, *navvies* for short, formed the backbone of the workforce that forced its way through Britain's fields to build the canal and railway network. And in the 19th century the men of the Ulster spade mills turned out different spades to meet the different demands of local soils and local traditions. Since the Irish gardener was said to have trod his spade with the right foot and the Englishman his left, both types were manufactured. In fact there were more than a hundred different spades, from the thin, bladed 'loys' of southern and western Ireland to the solid two-shouldered Ulster digging spade. There were mud spades and drain spades, trench spades and peat-cutting slanes, each fitted with its springy and shock-absorbing ash handle.

But the spade alone was not enough to manage the field crops. There was weeding to be done with a hoe, a forked stick, or a hook 'ground sharpe both behind and before,' as John Fitzherbert recommended in his 16th-century *Book of Husbandrie*. Corn and hay was cut with a hook; the design, like that of any other tool prior to the Industrial Revolution, varied from country to country, even from village to village. Working the woods, 'by hook and by crook', for field stakes, poles and canes involved, in England alone, more than 25 different designs of bill hook.

The sickle was the specialist's harvest tool, as handy for topping large quantities of beet for cattle feed as for clearing grass. Constant whetting with the sharpening stone would grind down the blade of the field worker's favourite tool until it resembled the cusp of a new moon.

The sickle's big brother came into its own to harvest the hay or cut the corn, when 'the mower whets his scythe' as the poet Milton put it in his *L'Allegro*. And so for centuries have these and other basic hand tools, the East African *panga*, the hay rake, the Javanese rice knife or *ani-ani*, and the sugar-cane-cutting *machete* served in the field.

SUGAR CANE

Name: Sugar cane
(*Saccharum*)

What it's like: A tropical grass, the sugar cane grows into a 3-metre (10-foot), bamboo-like stalk. The sugar cane's photosynthesis results in the plant storing sucrose in the sap, which is extracted to produce raw sugar. Having yielded its sugars, which are also used in the manufacture of ethanol fuel and alcohol, the spent canes or *bagasse* are turned into biodegradable materials for paper and cardboard, or burned as fuel to generate electricity.

Sugar cane was first grown in Asia, cane sugar being reportedly used in India 5,000 years ago. It was introduced to Africa and the Mediterranean countries by Arab traders, but there were bitter consequences to its introduction to the Americas: the sugar cane estates became central to the black slave economy.

Around half of the world's crop is still cut by hand. The cane plantations are often first set alight to burn off the dried leaves and break down the waxy coating on the plant stems. Hand- or machine-cut canes must be processed quickly in mills as the cane's sugar content degenerates rapidly after cutting.

Where it's grown: Brazil is the world's largest sugar-cane grower, followed by India. However, the crop is grown in almost 200 countries, in fact, more or less anywhere with a tropical or sub-tropical climate.

Mr. Foljambe's Plough

It's said that farmers find it difficult to drive in a straight line. Constantly preoccupied by how their neighbours' fields are faring, they cannot help looking from side to side as they drive by. 'You'd be careful to keep a straight furrow', recalled one old ploughman, 'for there was sure to be someone watching you over the hedge.' In the 18th century the biggest preoccupation was the plough.

Early ploughs, handmade by the village carpenter, were designed to be drawn by ox, horse or the farmer himself, with a share to cut into the soil and create a furrow, and a breast or moldboard to turn the soil. The plough was a significant improvement on hand tools such as the mattock and spade, and did a fine job of cultivating light soils. A heavy loam, however, caused problems. Requiring extra teams of up to six horses to pull the plough, a heavy clay soil could cause the plough to sink into the ground or veer wildly off the furrow.

By the 1700s farmers in England were craning their necks over the hedgerows to catch a glimpse of the Rotherham plough. Never mind the Kentish turn-wrest, the Hertfordshire wheel, the Norfolk gallows or the traditional Devonshire, the Rotherham was the Cadillac of the fields. Built by Joseph Foljambe of Rotherham – he had improved on a Dutch-designed plough and patented his version in 1730 – it set farmers gossiping over its lightweight construction and streamlined good looks. In America George Washington was impressed by the plough: 'I sent to England for what was then called the Rotherham or patent plough; and, till it began to wear and was ruined by a bungling country smith, no plough could have done better work', he wrote to one London merchant. Its technical breakthrough was having the three key parts of the coulter, the share and the breast or moldboard, all mounted on a single, rigid triangular frame.

> 'I sent to England for what was then called the Rotherham or patent plough; and, till it began to wear and was ruined by a bungling country smith, no plough could have done better work.'
>
> George Washington, in a letter to Arthur Young, 1786

Mann's Patent Improved Plough was one of a host of new-fangled ploughs that was unleashed upon the farming market in the 18th and 19th centuries.

The design would dictate the shape of the plough for the next century and a half. Most farmers, however, could only afford to look at it and sigh: the plough was the most expensive piece of equipment on any farm and the Rotherham was no exception. But Mr. Foljambe had a bright idea for making his radical invention affordable: mass production. Foljambe anticipated the central feature of the 19th-century Industrial Revolution, factory-style production, by a hundred years. He set himself and his workers up in the town of Rotherham – hence the plough's name – where standard wooden parts could be duplicated from his master patterns. At the peak of production Foljambe's factory was turning out an impressive 300 ploughs a year.

There were more remarkable inventions to come. When iron-foundry masters discovered that molten iron could be 'cast', or poured, into a mould rather than having to be beaten, or 'wrought', into shape on an anvil, cheap, cast-iron ploughs put the plough carpenter out of business. England was now at the forefront of the world's agricultural revolution and it was its eastern counties, Norfolk, Suffolk, Essex and Leicestershire, that were in the vanguard.

Robert Ransome built a foundry at the port of Ipswich in Suffolk in 1789 so that he could export the mainstay of his business, farm ploughs that even came with replaceable spare parts. Business boomed. In 1841 the Ransome family firm exhibited the first portable steam engine at the Royal Agricultural Show. A static machine, it had to be hauled around by teams of farm horses, but it heralded another step forward until the following year when Ransome introduced the first self-propelled agricultural steam engine.

The 'steamers' were too heavy to draw a plough, although one John Fowler invented a method of dragging the plough across the field by ropes attached to a leviathan steam engine. Another method was to station a steamer at either side of the field and haul the plough between them. The arrival of the tractor-mounted plough saw an end to the steam engine and the horse, especially with the development of the clever hydraulic lift that raised the plough clear of the ground at the headland, and having turned, dropped it ready for the next furrow. The design of the plough itself harked back to the 'turn-wrest', first used in the 1700s. Perhaps no sight was more remarkable to the distracted farmer than the first glimpse of a Rotherham as it sliced effortlessly through the heavier clay soils.

Seed Fiddles and Drills

Farmer Edward Abell strode out across his field, working his seed fiddle like a walking cellist. The 80-year-old was demonstrating to a film crew how, as a boy in the 1930s, he used to sow seed by hand with his Aerobroadcast seed fiddle. The seed fiddle had cost a few shillings: his latest John Deere tractor, parked in the field behind him, had cost £75,000. 'I could seed a ten-acre [four-hectare] grass field in a day with the Aerobroadcaster,' he told the film crew. 'I can do ten acres in an hour with the John Deere.' But Edward Abell's seed fiddle was already 200 years out of date when he started using it, for Jethro Tull had come up with a mechanical sowing device in the 18th century.

Tull, an English gentleman farmer born in Berkshire in 1674, was looking forward to a legal career. But he was distracted after touring Europe to study farming. He returned determined to improve yields on his father's Oxfordshire farm. Once he moved to his own Prosperous Farm near Hungerford he watched his farm labourers sowing seed by hand. The seed was sown in straight furrows to make harvesting easier, but much of the expensive seed, sown too close together, was wasted. Tull tried to persuade the men to sow more slowly and accurately. When they failed to do so, he designed a machine to replace them.

Designed to be drawn by a horse and to drop one seed at a time in three parallel furrows, his drill resembled a complicated wheelbarrow. Seeds fell from a seed box and rolled into a hopper where they were dispensed one by one in front of a coulter that drew the soil back over the furrow.

'It was named a drill,' he explained, 'because when farmers want to sow their beans and peas into channels or furrows by hand they call the action drilling.'

His machine was not the first, the best or even the most efficient of its kind. So why does the Jethro Tull seed drill spring to mind when anyone mentions agricultural innovation? Similar machines had been invented elsewhere in Europe and many suffered from similar problems: uneven ground caused havoc, wet ground even more so. But Tull's drill offered something more. The farmer was also the village church organist and he adapted the mechanisms of the organ stops to devise his unique, single-seed dispenser. He had a second advantage: he was a good publicist. Detailed plans for his drill were printed in his *Horse Hoeing Husbandry*, published in 1733, eight years before his death. By then he had improved his drill, and while arguments about the merits of his system continued for a century after his book's publication, the rudiments of the Jethro Tull seed drill proved themselves in the passage of time.

Farmhouse and Granary

The field and the farmhouse are inextricably linked. The farmer cannot manage without either. The earliest permanent structure was either a temple or a farm dwelling, and given the need for warmth before worship, the farmhouse probably came first. Yet the word *farmhouse* came relatively late in history: *farm*, from the Latin *firma*, signified a fixed payment, rent or lease and referred to a parcel of land let, or 'farmed out' by the landowner.

The farmhouse, barn and granary were traditionally built with whatever lay close to hand – stone, timber, bamboo – and in wet climates given a weatherproof finish of clapboard or mud and limewash. Sometimes only the barn and farmhouse door were picked out in white to help the farmer find his way home in the dark. The homegrown, vernacular style (*vernacular* comes from the Latin for a slave born in his master's house and thus a local 'product') has patterned the countrysides around the world. Where there was nothing better with which to build, or where the people were too poor to purchase materials, the earth itself was put to use: Adobe, pisé, tapia, cob and clom have been used across the world in Asia, Africa, South America and Europe.

Pisé, for example, was introduced to southern Europe by the Romans. The method involved forming a foundation of rubble or brick and then throwing a

mix of sand and gravel with a little clay to bind the dirt, down between wooden shuttering boards. The earthy grit was pounded down with a wooden pole or iron rod to remove any air pockets, and sometimes broken glass was added to the mix, supposedly to dissuade rats and mice from tunnelling through the walls. A man could build up to his own height in a day, provided the rain, which could wash away a day's work in minutes, stayed away. Wood or brick frames were set in the walls for doors and windows and a roof was added with broad eaves to protect the walls. The pisé was waterproofed with a layer of clay and painted with copious quantities of whitewash or decorated with geometric patterns.

In some places a skirting coat of tar was painted around the base of the walls, partly to deter farm animals from licking away at the natural salts oozing out, partly to protect them from the splashing rain, and partly because that was the way it had always been done.

The farmhouse was the farmer's finest tool. It provided the family with a home, a hearth – the introduction of the chimney was almost as revolutionary as the invention of the plough – bier, barn and field store rolled into one. The threshold was set between opposing doors so that the draft would help blow the chaff from the grain. And, until they were sent out into their own quarters, the farm animals were stabled inside.

'At his bed's feete feeden his stalled teame, The swine beneath, his pullen o'er the beame' wrote the 17th-century Bishop Joseph Hall. When Mr. William Bingley took his lunch in a Welsh farmhouse during a walk through that country in 1798 he was in the company of the farmer, his wife 'and a large, overgrown old sow devouring her dinner with considerable dissatisfaction on account of short allowance, from a pail placed for her by the daughter in one corner of the room.'

In the early days grain yields were so small than most of the grain was milled right away and the little that was left, precious seed corn for the following year, was kept in the farmhouse. However, as yields improved, more sophisticated granaries were required.

In the Minho region of Portugal the stone granaries, or *espigueiros*, carrying a Christian cross for protection over the doorway, were built on mushroom-shaped 'staddle' stones to prevent rats from reaching the grain inside. Similarly

A grain silo in Indiana is characteristic of the tall and imposing silos that can be found in the United States and Canada; however, grain is stored in many different ways around the world.

the ancient thatched *hórreos*, the corn stores of Galicia and Asturias in Spain, were so elaborate that many pilgrims making their way to the shrine at Santiago de Compostela mistook them for religious hermitages. In Niger, West Africa, pots for storing millet were made like giant earthenware vessels, while in Canada and the United States it was the towering grain silo that punctuated the skyline.

Mills and Millers

'The farmer is the man who feeds us all,' goes the traditional song of the American Midwest. In truth it was the millers who had mastered the earliest industrial processes with their water- or wind-powered mills that could grind corn. Generations down the line it was the millers who founded some of the wealthiest dynasties of the Industrial Revolution and eventually multinational corporations such as Associated British Foods, Cargill and Unilever.

The early wind-powered mills were built in the Middle East in the seventh century and the technology was taken by crusader knights back to Europe where, up until then, the watermill had predominated.

Watermills were set on the upper reaches of rivers, where the water ran swift-est, or on the lower reaches where a large quantity of water could be channelled to provide free energy. Some were sited on the coast, driven by seawater trapped in special reservoirs at high tide. The mill wheel was either set below the mill – the ancient invention was known as a click mill – or to one side of the mill.

Gradually the watermill was superseded by the more efficient windmill. The typical 19th-century smock windmill – so named because it looked so much like the field worker's traditional overgarment or smock – had four canvas-covered sails, which turned in the wind, a fantail at the rear of the revolving cap at its summit turning the sails to face the best of the breeze. The canvas sails at which Miguel de Cervantes's misguided Don Quixote had tilted – he mistook them for giants because, Cervantes explained in *Don Quixote de la Mancha*, 'the moisture of his brain was exhausted' – were eventually replaced by hinged wooden shutters, sophisticated devices that could self-adjust according to the strength of the wind. The sails turned a geared shaft that drove the millstones below.

Preparing the millstones was a skilled and specialised craft. There were French burr stones from the Marne, built from sections of hard quartz bound together with a ring of iron, and complete stones cut from a single piece of millstone grit quarried in Derbyshire, England. The stones were grooved or furrowed to better grind the grain and channel the flour off the stones into the miller's sacks. As the stones wore away the millstone dresser would be called to dress them again. Dressing the hard stones left the stone dresser's hands embedded with metal splinters from his mill bill, prompting the expression to 'show your mettle', in other words to show your experience or true worth. In non-mechanised communities it was, and still is, the hand-turned *quern* that served the families' needs.

The Blacksmith

There was a time when, aside from the mosque or church, and the village bar, there was one other popular meeting place in the parish: the smithy. On a winter's evening villagers were drawn to the light and warmth of the forge like moths to a candle. 'He earns whate'er he can, And looks the whole world in the face, For he owes not any man,' wrote Henry Longfellow in his 1841 poem *The Village Blacksmith*. The blacksmith could shoe the farm horse, mend the broken plough, make a gate hinge, and if the yeoman was sufficiently wealthy make him a metal memorial for the graveyard – perhaps turning to the local schoolmistress for assistance with his spelling.

The smith was more properly a forgemaster, for his work revolved around the forge where he took pig iron – the first product of the iron-making process – and shaped it to the farmers' needs.

One American blacksmith who, had he survived for two centuries, would perhaps have been surprised to have found his name emblazoned across the globe, was born in Rutland, Vermont, in 1804. After an elementary schooling he

'Consider, sir,' answered Sancho, 'that those which appear yonder, are not giants, but windmills; and what seems arms are sails, which, whirled around by the wind, make the millstone go.'

Miguel de Cervantes, *Don Quixote de la Mancha*, 1605

dutifully served his four-year apprenticeship as a blacksmith and by the age of 21 had gained a reputation for the quality of his hayforks and shovels. The trouble was, no one could afford them. So in 1836 the young man, John Deere, leaving his wife and children behind to join him later, set out for the West, where, it was said, fortunes were being made. Within two days of arriving in Grand Detour, Illinois, he had built a forge and was busy serving the local farmers.

From them he learned of the serious problem they encountered in trying to farm the fertile soils of the Midwest. Their cast-iron ploughs were designed for the light, sandy New England soils of the east, not the rich Midwestern soil which clogged up the plough. Ploughing was slow and laboured as the plough-man had to keep stopping to scrape the soil from the shares.

In 1873 Deere devised a self-scouring plough made with steel from a broken saw blade, successfully testing it on a farm nearby. He started manufacturing his self-polishing ploughs from special rolled steel he shipped from England and was soon producing 1,000 ploughs a year. By the time his son, Charles, who had taken on the business, died in 1907, the one-time blacksmith shop was making ploughs, cultivators and corn and cotton planters. The John Deere tractors were yet to come (see page 163).

Across the world the blacksmith continued servicing the needs of the field worker. 'Each morning sees some task begin, Each evening sees it close; Something attempted, something done, Has earned a night's repose,' wrote Longfellow, painting a pastoral picture of life around the forge. But historically there was a dark side to the business of forging chains for agriculture. William Hutton, a businessman from Birmingham, England, was walking through Walsall town in 1741 when he was arrested by the sight of half-naked women slaving over their anvils. 'I observed one, or more females, stript of their upper garments and not overcharged with the lower, wielding the hammer with all the grace of their sex.'

What was essentially a form of industrial slavery was still going on in 1896 when Robert Sherard wrote in *Pearson's Magazine*: 'No part of this work is work for women, and his manhood is ashamed who sees these poor female beings swinging their heavy hammers or working the treadles of the Oliver.' The Oliver was a treadle hammer, named after the famously heavy-handed English Civil War leader, Oliver Cromwell.

Sherard wrote of one girl apprenticed to a chain maker and making chain harrows for the farm. 'She was fourteen by the Factory Act: by paternity she was ten, I never saw such little arms, and her hands were made to cradle dolls.'

Despite the conditions the girl was singing. 'I also saw her owner approach with a clenched fist and heard him say: "I'll give you 'some golden hair was hanging down her back!' Why don't you get on with your work!"' Sherard's exposé of the sufferings of those he described as 'the white slaves of England' eventually helped to bring the business to an end.

Show Time

From the Homowo Festival of Ghana, West Africa (*homowo* translates as 'hooting at hunger'), to the Balinese crop festival, Nyepi, and from Southern India's Pongal rice-harvest festival to the Christian Harvest Festival, harvest is a time for celebration. Whether the celebration marked the first pressing of the olives or grapes, or the final weigh-in of the hops or sugar cane, it was an excuse for a big meal, much toasting, and the possibility of a spring-born baby or two.

The harvest also gave farmers the chance to show off their successes in the field. The third President of the United States, Thomas Jefferson, at Monticello, his estate in Virginia, liked to compete with his neighbours over who would grow the first crop of peas fit for the plate. The competition was usually won by a Mr. George Divers who then had the privilege of throwing the celebration dinner, peas included.

This spirit of competition had a place in the annual farm show too, as trestle tables were hauled out, covered in linen, and used to showcase the best of the local crops and crafts. There were curious competitions for the best mangel-wurzel, bacon rasher or square of grass turf, or for the cleverest sheep dog, ugliest vegetable or best-dressed scarecrow. And there was another element to these agricultural shows: demonstrations. The blacksmith might show off his new range of hedge slashers, the skep maker her latest straw bee skep, the basket weaver his new line in calf muzzles.

The agricultural show gradually grew into a major event occupying whole farms for a weekend and attracting showmen, fairgrounds, travelling theatre groups and farm-machinery agents. The farm show gave agricultural-machinery manufacturers the opportunity to exhibit their latest hoes, drills, hay makers and mechanical threshers. Injecting a little prize money into the proceedings for a ploughing match or hedging competition oiled the wheels of their progress.

The agricultural fête, fiesta or fair still has a place in every country's calendar, but the year 1851 saw London launch the biggest showcase for agricultural machinery ever seen: the Great Exhibition. England under Queen Victoria in the 1850s remained the world's leading agricultural nation – largely thanks to the absence of any armed conflict on its soil after 1650. During her 64-year reign from 1837 to 1901, Victoria ruled a quarter of the globe and one in four of the people on it. Her reign would see the transformation of the field and the tools that turned it, and in 1851 her husband, Prince Albert, organised the Great Exhibition in the specially built Crystal Palace to prove it.

Six million people with money to spend descended on the Palace to marvel at more than 100,000 exhibits including the very latest farm machines. There were chaff-cutting engines, linseed-cake crushers, turnip cutters, ploughs, hoppers, winnowers, 'improved' hay makers, liquid-manure dispensers, clod crushers, rollers, expandable lever harrows, and a 'two-horse-power' thrashing machine with bevel gearwork. One firm offered eight different wheelbarrows and no fewer than 28 different carts for carrying manure.

One 18-year-old, however, threw away his exhibition ticket, boycotting the show because in his view it had been hijacked by industrialists. It was the young William Morris, who went on to play a crucial role in the Arts and Crafts movement. 'Forget the snorting steam and piston stroke, Forget the spreading of the hideous town; Think rather of the pack-horse on the down, And dream of London, small and white and clean,' Morris wrote in *The Earthly Paradise* between 1868 and 1870.

The Great Exhibition also marked the beginning of the end for British supremacy in the field, for there was plenty of foreign promise among the exhibits, especially from the United States. Cyrus Hall McCormick and Obed Hussey sent along their reaping machines, while Nathaniel Clayton and Joseph Shuttleworth's 'combined thrashing, straw shaking, riddling, and winnowing machine (with wood wheels, £55 for the 3 Horse version)' caused quite a stir.

'Forget the snorting steam and piston stroke,
Forget the spreading of the hideous town;
Think rather of the pack-horse on the down,
And dream of London, small and white and clean.'

William Morris, *The Earthly Paradise*, 1868–70

Machines can break, however, and the one certain source of power in the field is the farmer's muscle. Beasts of burden had their part to play, too, but everything from milking the house cow to grinding the corn can be done with the dextrous hand. In 1871 some 75 per cent of the British harvest was still cut by hand and the situation was much the same across Europe. The Americans were about to take the lead in demonstrating just how much more one pair of hands could do.

From Horse to Steam

The ox-drawn plough could be up to 3,500 years old or more, but the trudging draft horse did not impact on the fields of Europe until the 1700s when Ransome's all-iron plough, Tull's seed drill, and other new-fangled farm machinery began to appear. The generally docile, if sometimes truculent, donkey, descended from the asses of Africa and Asia, continued to serve his masters and mistresses, especially in the Adriatic countries: in the mid-1990s there were still thought to be about a quarter of a million donkeys competing with that other popular form of Aegean rural transport, the wheelbarrow.

The farm horse could out-pull the ox. One wagoner recalled the impatient strength of one farm mare: 'Once she called to pull she pulled no matter what. One time this mare's traces was snagged round a granite gate post and she did heave 'til she fell dead of a heart attack.' The horse could operate the treadmill – one Belgian invention allowed corn to be threshed on such a treadmill-powered device – or tow half a metric ton of turnips loaded in a two-wheeled *tumbril*, or cart. It could respond to instructions, as our wagoner recalled, with unfortunate results. But a shepherd who continued working with horses into the 1960s reported that when he was feeding roots to his winter flock he could tell the horse when to move on. 'Try doing that with a tractor.' Some horses were even smart enough to know when they were dealing with a beginner. 'I started ploughing at the age of eleven,' remembered one ploughboy. 'They seemed to know they had a novice at the traces and responded accordingly.' Fuelled on hay, grass and oats, heavy horses would continue to serve their masters for their average 20-year lifespan.

When steam machines started to appear 200 years ago, there seemed to be no competition. Even the invention of Scotsman Andrew Meikle's corn-threshing machine in 1786 – the grain was threshed between rollers rather than having to be threshed manually with 'crab tree' or threshing sticks – was horse-driven. By the mid-1800s such a horse-driven machine could thresh seven metric tons in a day, 28 times what a man could manage. But when the first of the contractor's steam-threshing machines rolled into the farmyard, the farmer found the 'steamer' was managing 25 metric tons in a day. The draft horse's days were numbered.

Once gearing, which allowed the steam machine's power to be transferred from its belt drives to its wheels, had been introduced, the horse was no longer needed to haul it from farm to farm. Instead these shiny leviathans, billowing steam, scared the farm dogs and made small boys stop and stare in wonder. The 'General Purpose Agricultural Engine' could not only drive a threshing machine, it could operate the new straw balers and clover hullers and haul previously unimagined payloads. Their strength, to add insult to injury from an equine point of view, was measured in horse power and official ratings of 12 to 14 horse power often concealed a true power four or five times greater.

There was one drawback: farm accidents not only increased in number, but in severity – the consequences of catching a limb in the traces of a haulage horse bore no comparison to those of slipping down into the whipping belt of a threshing machine.

As late as the 1930s there were still 40,000 dray horses operating in Greater London alone, but by now the number of horses in the field had fallen by 35 per cent. The tractors, when they arrived, replaced between two and four dray horses each. By 1947, there were half a million horses working the fields of England, but they were being killed off at the rate of 100,000 a year.

The Tractor

Nikolaus Otto, born at Holzhausen, Germany, in 1832, was a man full of ideas. One of them concerned the atmospheric engine, a machine free from steam power, fuelled with gas and capable of driving a piston in a cylinder. In Otto's four-stroke engine the piston sucked in fuel on the first stroke, compressed it on the second, was driven into its third as the fuel was ignited by a spark, and blew out the spent

The modern tractor revolutionised farming more than any other single machine, and saw the final days of draft horses working the fields.

fuel, or exhaust, on the fourth. Gottlieb Daimler and Wilhelm Maybach decided this was a work of genius and entered into partnership with him.

Most 19th-century farmers, still dependent on their hired hands and horses, could see little future in these static, gas-powered engines, although some saved on their wages by running them as they had the steam engines, to power other farm machines. But in the 1880s an American, John Charter, unveiled a curious-looking machine. Considerably lighter than the old steam engines, it was powered by liquid fuel and was based on Otto's prototype four-stroke engine. It was going to change the face of farming forever. It was called a traction engine, or 'tractor' for short.

The tractor would, over the next century and a quarter, nibble away at village populations around the world: every time a farmer traded in his horses for a tractor the number of people living and working in the fields fell. In the United States at the start of the 1940s there were 1.2 million tractors and 6.8 million people on the farms; a decade later there were almost four times as many tractors. The farm population meanwhile had fallen by almost two-thirds.

Change did not happen overnight, but by 1915 fourteen tractor companies had opened shop in Illinois, including Charter's and the former blacksmith John Deere's. A few years earlier an Irishman named Harry Ferguson started importing American tractors and selling them from his hometown, Belfast in Northern Ireland. Here the horse, ox and donkey still reigned supreme as beasts of burden. Grain was still sown, cut, carried and threshed by hand. Firewood and fodder was either transported behind horse- or donkey-drawn vehicles – they ranged from the basic slide car, a sled with shafts, to the farm cart – or carried on the smallholder's back with 'burden ropes' made from straw or hay. Baskets of turf were carried on the head, cushioned on a ring of hay, the *fáinne*.

By 1914 Europe was embroiled in the First World War and governments were desperate to replace the man and horse power that had been sent to the battlefield. The British government ordered in American farm tractors including, in 1917, a sturdy little machine that was still in prototype, the Fordson. The clever thing about the Fordson was that it had no frame; or rather its essential elements, the engine, gearbox and rear axle, when joined together, created the frame. The Fordson was cheap, strong and light enough to cross a field without becoming bogged down by its own weight. It could plough at 4.5 kilometres per hour (2.8 miles per hour), weighed just over a metric ton, and could carve up 3 hectares (8 acres) on a single tank of paraffin.

While chunky crawler tractors, which ran on caterpillar tracks rather than wheels, still sold well to farmers with a heavy soil to cultivate, the four-wheeled tractor was set to usurp the horse, the ox, the water buffalo and the steam engine. In the 1930s Harry Ferguson was proudly demonstrating what sounded like a complicated device, a hydraulic lift and three-point linkage – in fact it was a piece of engineering brilliance which, mounted on the back of the 'Fergie', performed like mechanical biceps, lifting equipment clear of the ground. Neither ploughs, small carts nor a host of other farm implements needed wheels any longer.

In 1939 Europe was plunged into the Second World War. Again millions of farm workers were sent away to fight; and again those that were left behind found themselves short of food and the mechanical means to sow, grow and harvest it. When the war ended Britain, one of the few non-neutral European countries to have escaped enemy occupation, had the most highly mechanised agricultural industry in the world.

As the developed nations rumbled towards a total transformation of farming, there were a number of teething problems. More than a few novice tractor drivers came to grief shouting at the little machine to 'whoa' instead of applying the brake. And it was even said that a tractor or two attracted the unwelcome attention of the amorous – if somewhat short-sighted – bull. But tractors such as the Fordson, which by the 1940s commanded 90 per cent of the UK market, turned out to be mighty monsters as happy hauling peat or potatoes as they were carrying the family, balanced on the mudguards, to school and church. Within just a generation the stable, the cart shed and the wagon shed had become redundant buildings.

It was all thanks to Nikolaus Otto. Or was it? Five years before Otto's death in 1891, the patent office revoked his patent. The four-stroke engine, it seems, had already been invented by the French engineer Alphonse Beau de Rochas.

From Field to Freezer

Until the invention of the freezer and chiller, the only way to buy food fresh from the field was at market. But the market was changing.

The change began at harvest time in the 1920s, when a curious contraption started to appear in the American vegetable fields. Mounted on the back of a truck, the machine was designed to fast-freeze the field crop by way of metal plates that had been cooled to –40°C (–40°F) with calcium chloride brine.

It had been developed and patented by a tenacious entrepreneur, Clarence (Bob to his friends) Birdseye, an inventor who, unlike his many sceptics, was convinced that, one day, people would want to buy food that had been frozen to preserve it. And vegetables, thought Bob, needed to be frozen fast and fresh.

He had learned the art of freezing food from native north Canadians when, as a fur trapper in Labrador in the early 1900s, he, his wife Eleanor, and their son shared a three-roomed cabin 250 miles away from the nearest store. Bob Birdseye learned what the native north Canadians already knew, that meat tasted better if it was fast-frozen. Fish, rabbit, duck and other game, naturally frozen outdoors in the Arctic winds that drove temperatures down to a perishing −50°C (−58°F), kept its flavour. 'The Eskimos had used it for centuries. What I accomplished … was merely to make packaged frozen food available to the public,' he would say later.

The business of freezing food straight from the field was not new. The ice house was a fashionable must-have among the European nobility three centuries earlier. Charles II of England had an ice house built in St. James's Park in 1600. Built of stone or brick and set in the ground, the pit of the house was filled with ice, cut from a handy, neighbouring lake during the winter. Packed down, the ice kept for twelve months or more. The chamber above was lined with rails and used to store vegetables, game and other meats. If the estate owners imagined their ice houses to be the coolest of modern conveniences they had forgotten about Alexander the Great, who was said to have filled trenches at Petra with mountain snow in the summer and, covering them with branches, stored his soldiers' wine, fruit and vegetables within.

Bob Birdseye continued to experiment with fast-freezing vegetables, placing cabbages in barrels of water that could be hacked out of the ice when required. When the family returned to the United States in 1917 he tried to re-create the Labrador winters with ice blocks, brine and electric fans in the corner of an ice cream factory in New Jersey. The business went bust.

The Birdseyes moved to a fishing port, Gloucester, Massachusetts, where Bob set up the General Seafoods Company and where he continued to experiment with quick-freezing food. Business was slow and he and Eleanor had already hocked their insurance policies when their fortunes changed suddenly. Bob Birdseye was about to receive $22 million, then the largest sum of money ever paid for a single process.

The pay-off came when the wealthy daughter of a food-processing company owner, Marjorie Merriweather Post, was holidaying on her yacht off the Massachusetts coast. One evening her chef served up roast goose purchased earlier in Gloucester from the Birdseyes' General Seafoods Company. When Post learned that the fresh goose was actually several months old, she made an appointment to see the inventor. Three years later her family firm bought out Bob Birdseye and in 1930 changed the name to Birds Eye.

Now millionaires, Bob and Eleanor retired to indulge their passion for horticulture. Bob was interested in the emerging 'field-free' growing technique of hydroponics and believed that the flat roofs and cellars of New York were sufficient to grow all the city needed in the way of fresh vegetables. But for the new company business was a struggle. The frozen product might have revolutionised the processing of fresh vegetables, but shopkeepers still had to be persuaded to make room for a frozen-food cabinet in their store and housewives persuaded to buy a home freezer.

By now some commentators predicted that shoppers would one day buy their food, fresh or frozen, not at a dozen different market stalls, but from a central 'store' with butcher, greengrocer, delicatessen and fish shop all under one roof. It would never catch on, retorted the food writers. After all, who would ever want to eat frozen peas at Christmas? Or 'fresh' fish that was at least six months old? Only time would tell.

Chapter Seven

NATURE'S
BOUNTY

Cereal grains such as rice, corn and wheat provide a staggeringly high proportion of the total food intake of the world's population, with just those three accounting for 43 per cent of the calories we eat. However, if you know what you are looking for, even wild meadows offer a huge range of foods to collect and eat, most of which have formed a vital part of people's diets for centuries. Here is a guide to some of what's good and what's not.

Living off the Land

Everyone on the planet lives off the land, although we all have different degrees of direct engagement. For instance, a Sumatran housewife shopping at a roadside stall for green leaves to supplement the evening meal of rice will be more aware of the origins of her family's food than a student in Stockholm, trawling the shelves of a supermarket late at night. A New Zealand smallholder, engaged in raising organic meat and vegetables, will have a different view of the land from the backyard gardener with a few rows of vegetables, herbs and flowers.

It is difficult to appreciate just how dependent we are on plants. We rely on them not simply for food and to fatten the animals on which we feed, but also for medicines, cosmetics, oils, fabrics, cork, timber, rubber and much more. It is an impressive list. Every time we ride in a car, sit at our desk, step into a shopping centre, visit the pharmacist, the doctor or the dentist, use household paint, brush the kitchen floor with a wooden-handled broom, or open the cork of a wine bottle, we use some part of a plant.

Plants are divided into *angiosperms*, or flowering plants with 'enclosed' seeds – they form by far the largest group with well over 400,000 different species; *gymnosperms* with 'naked' seeds, such as conifers; and non-seed-bearing plants such as ferns, mosses and algae.

Each species is specially adapted to living off the land or water. As well as the more obvious flowers of the field margins such as the common white or ox-eye

On the margins of a field a complex variety of plants can be found. This pattern repeats itself the world over, as wild plants exploit the niches that humans leave untended.

daisy, there are snow-proof shrubs sheltering in Alpine regions, salt-proof sedges clinging to sea shores, and cacti and spurges eking out a precarious existence in the desert. There are plants such as the Mediterranean bee orchid that mimic the female of certain insects to reproduce, and plants such as the burdock or 'sticky bob' that evolved spiny seed cases that attach themselves to the fur of passing mammals so they spread themselves far and wide. There are plants with mucus-covered seeds, such as mistletoe – William Turner helpfully explained in his 1532 *Herbal* how the mistletoe was carried from one tree to another as 'the thrush shiteth out the micel berries' – and plants such as sundews that eat insects to survive.

The richest and most complex plant communities are those of the rainforests that once encircled the earth's equatorial zone. There may be as many as 90,000 different species in Central and South America, 30,000 in Africa, and a remarkable 9,500 on the world's fourth-largest island, Madagascar. No one knows the true number: more are being discovered although, with the current levels of rainforest destruction, many will become extinct before we have the chance to find them. Temperate zones have fewer species, but are no less important – the Mediterranean region, for example, hosts around 5,000 species.

All plants are essential to our life on land, and the wild margins of the field represent a genetic bank. The vegetables of today sprang from the wilderness, parsnip, beetroot, carrot – which came in from the wild in a rainbow-like range of colours ranging from scarlet and purple to white and yellow – the wild cabbage (*Brassica oleracea*) brought into cultivation by Moors, Greeks and Italians, and asparagus, first grown in the fertile regions around the Nile and Indus. (Venetian farmers around Bassano were growing cultivated asparagus in the 1500s.)

Plants give off oxygen – marine algae account for over 50 per cent of that – as they convert carbon dioxide and water into carbohydrates, taking carbon from the air and passing it on to the food chain and back into the soil. Plants harvest phosphorus, potassium, calcium, magnesium and other trace elements from the soil, which are taken into the food chain from where, through animal manures and decomposition, they are returned to enrich the soil. Certain plants, mainly the leguminous peas and beans, feed the earth by 'fixing' nitrogen with the help of microbial organisms.

In the 10,000 years that we have lived off the field, plants have kept this cycle of life stable. But inexorably the field is not just reflecting the plants we use, but changing the plant world itself. Destroying forests to create new fields and burning fossil fuels to cultivate them increases carbon dioxide levels, which, in

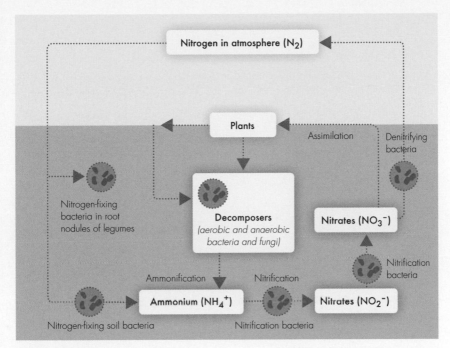

The nitrogen cycle is a crucial part of the nutrient cycle. Much of the nitrogen consumed by a plant is used to make chlorophyll, which in turn is used for photosynthesis.

turn, causes climate change. A sobering demonstration of the speed of this change can be seen at the Franz Joseph glacier in New Zealand, where marker posts signal the annual, and all-too-rapid, retreat of the ice.

In the last 2,000 years most of the natural vegetation has been replaced by the managed vegetation of the fields. Too often it has been mismanaged: overdrained, overgrazed or simply replaced with field crops that eventually prove to be unsustainable.

If we are to live off the land we must have fertile soil. And plants play a fundamental role in stabilising the soil. A graphic example of how human interference can render a soil infertile was the 1930s Dust Bowl of the American Midwest, when the natural grassland was replaced with crops fed only on fertilisers. Without humus, decomposed organic matter that stabilises the soil and helps it hold water, the soil dried up and simply blew away. Thousands of farmers were forced to give up the land.

Such a calamity prompted politicians to think seriously about the way in which civilisations exploited their natural resources. Yet human intervention has

'When men lack a sense of awe, there will be disaster'

Lao Tsu, *Tao Te Ching*, sixth century B.C.E.

continued to damage an estimated third of the world's land, the semi-arid places where the natural plants – grass with scattered trees – are sustained by low rainfall under a harsh sun. Cutting down trees for use as firewood and over-grazing the grasslands eventually destroys the soil. Since the middle of the last century an area the size of China and India combined has suffered from this kind of soil deterioration.

If we are to continue living off the land, and feeding a growing world population, we must learn to appreciate field plants. 'When men lack a sense of awe, there will be disaster', predicts the sixth-century B.C.E. philosopher Lao Tsu in the *Tao Te Ching*.

Fruits and Berries

'What wondrous life is this I lead, Ripe apples drop about my head,' wrote an awestruck Andrew Marvell in his elegiac 1681 poem 'The Garden'.

Marvell's 'ripe apples' may have included an old French variety, *court pendu plat*, a light green fruit flushed with orange that was introduced to England in Marvell's time. It was one of the hardy descendants of the wild apple, a fruit that originated, and still grows, in southwest Asia on the Georgian, Iranian and Turkish borders. These ancient ancestors were brought into Europe and cultivated by the Greeks and Romans who, because the fruit did not breed true from seed, mastered the craft of grafting new varieties onto wild rootstocks. The *court pendu plat*, and another old variety, *pomme d'api*, most likely started life in a Roman orchard.

European monasteries carried the craft of grafting forward, most of their apple production being devoted to cider making, and helped make the apple (of the genus *Malus*) the most popular fruit of the temperate zone. The apple's popularity and the variety of species is reflected in the rich array of evocative names it has developed: catshead, leathercoat, democrat, Charles Ross, delicious,

Baldwin, Ben David, McIntosh – a key Canadian variety – striped beefing, Cheddar cross, Granny Smith – raised in Australia – and golden delicious – raised in America.

The Europeans introduced apple seeds rather than apple trees to America and the North American varieties developed a wider genetic stock as a consequence. They were assisted by the strange figure of John Chapman, a 19th-century itinerant apple-tree grower – he acquired his seeds free from cider mills – and preacher. Chapman became the American folk hero Johnny Appleseed and established apple nurseries all around Ohio, Indiana and Illinois.

'The nectarine, and curious peach, Into my hands themselves do reach,' continued Marvell. The nectarine had arrived in England from central and eastern Asia a generation earlier. His 'curious peach' was believed to have come from Persia (now Iran) – from where it derives its name – although it actually originated in China. The poet, however, made no mention of plums – probably derived from the damson (*Prunus institis*), cherry plum (*Prunus cerasifera*) or the blackthorn or sloe (*Prunus spinosa*) – nor the delicious papaya and pawpaw.

In India and East Africa the tropical papaya (*Carica papaya*) – confusingly sometimes referred to as the pawpaw, which is actually a different genus – could be pulped into a sweet fruit juice and the green fruit turned into pies. Even the stems were useful: they were cut and carved into children's flutes. The unrelated but similar pawpaw of the Americas, a different species in the genus *Asimina*, was more at home in America's Mississippi Valley. Aside from eating the fruit and cooking the leaves like spinach, the Native Americans discovered how to powder the seed to make a useful insecticide against head lice.

Many of the indigenous tropical fruits were taken into the plantation: the banana, date, citrus fruits such as oranges, lemons, mandarins, tangerines and limes, and the avocado – once a favourite native food of the jaguar. Nor did Marvell mention the pomelo, or 'Chinese grapefruit', native to Southeast Asia – the Tamils called it *bumblimass* – now grown in great quantities in America, China and southern Africa.

Then there was the pineapple (*Ananas comosus*), a strange fruit that grew, not on a tree, but as a swollen flower stem. Growers in colder northern countries were envious of these tropical riches, and fortunes were invested on cultivating the *pines*, as they were called. Pine growing had a lasting influence on the development of the glasshouse or conservatory, which developed firstly as a hothouse or pinery and later as 'a conservatory for tender plants ... and an entertaining room', as Shirley Hibberd wrote in *Profitable Gardening* (1884).

Yet temperate countries had their own rich stock of native fruits and berries. As the tree leaves turned in autumn, meadow margins and hedges offered rich pickings of wild plums and sloes, rowan (mountain ash) berries, crab apples that made a delicious deep-pink jelly, small wild cherries and rose hips. Some of the bush fruits taken into the field for cultivation, such as raspberries, black and red currants and gooseberries, escaped into the wild, and it's not unusual to find a colony of raspberries or currants growing on some woodland margin or the edge of a country lane.

Returning to the 'delicious solitude' of his Garden of Eden, Marvell wrote: 'Stumbling on melons, as I pass, Ensnared with flowers, I fall on grass.' The melon (*Cucumis melo*) belongs to the same family as the cucumber. It rose out of Africa and went on to be grown in India, China and Japan in an elongated form. But had Marvell stumbled on the ordinary melon or the watermelon (*Citrullus lanatus*)? This gargantuan fruit took the opposite route to the American pawpaw, starting out in Africa before travelling to India and then China in the 10th or 11th century. When it arrived in the Americas the watermelon was grown to gigantic proportions, over 250 pounds (113.4 kilograms) in one case.

The wise field worker, however, knew that size was not everything. The piquancy of a small but perfectly formed cloudberry picked along the Canadian Cabot Trail in Cape Breton Island, Nova Scotia, was hard to beat.

'What wondrous life is this I lead!
Ripe apples drop about my head;
The luscious clusters of the vine
Upon my mouth do crush their wine;
The nectarine and curious peach
Into my hands themselves do reach;
Stumbling on melons as I pass,
Ensnared with flowers, I fall on grass.'

Andrew Marvell, 'The Garden', 1681

DEWBERRY

Name: Dewberry
(*Rubus caesius*)

What it's like: More slender than the blackberry (see page 93) with smaller, less tightly packed fruit that have a typical white hue. Those growing in America have larger fruits than those of northern Europe. Its fruits, a blackish purple, are coated with a thin 'dew' of waxy droplets.

Other members of the *Rubus* genus are equally succulent. The cloudberry (*Rubus chamaemorus*), which produces large golden fruits used in jams and puddings, is a perennial with a creeping rhizome that produces thorn-free stems. In Canada, cloudberries are used to flavour a special beer; in Alaska they are made into 'Eskimo ice cream' mixed with seal oil or reindeer or caribou fat.

R. x loganobaccus, the loganberry, has dull red fruits, which are more acidic to the taste than those of the blackberry, but it produces them in much greater yields. Another relation, the raspberry (*R. idaeus*), was, according to the Victorian writer Shirley Hibberd, a 'useful fruit … but too often very carelessly grown, not by cottagers only, but by gardeners of some pretensions.'

Where it's grown: The dewberry is native to the United States, and John Budd wrote in his 1902 *American Horticultural Manual*: 'In different parts of the Union the trailing blackberry, or dewberry, runs into many forms or types, some of which have been decided to be – distinct species.' It is also common on lime-rich soils in Europe. Cloudberries are a plant of the open moorlands of Canada, northern Europe and the Arctic regions, while the loganberry, bred in California, is grown commercially, especially in America.

Herbs and Spices

A field hired out for a 'peppercorn rent' is let for an extremely low rent; but it was not always so. In medieval Europe black peppers were as scarce as hens' teeth. There was plenty of pepper in India, however. It grew in the berries of the Indian vine (*Piper nigrum*) and was widely used across the Indian subcontinent. But delivering it to Europe took months. Carried in the swaying saddle packs of horses and camels, the spice wound its slow way through India, Pakistan, over the Khyber Pass into Afghanistan, and on to Persia (now Iran), where it was shipped to the Mediterranean ports of Alexandria, Venice and Genoa. Fortunes were founded on its trade.

Pepper was originally called *poivrea* after the 18th-century French spice hunter Pierre Poivre. In Poivre's time the Dutch had monopolised the East Indies' spice trade, but Poivre managed to smuggle spice plants such as cloves and nutmeg out of the East Indies to Mauritius and Réunion in the Indian Ocean, where he was employed as the French administrator.

In the days before refrigeration, spices were vital, not only to preserve foods, but also to disguise unwelcome flavours. Other spices such as cinnamon, cardamom (or cardamon), caraway and turmeric were also grown in India and shipped abroad. In fact the country continues to produce more than 80 per cent of the world's spices.

South America had a pepper trade of its own (see page 181), and many people around the world have subsequently acquired a taste for fiery chilies. Contrary to popular belief, the seeds themselves carry no heat, and a chili's punch is actually a product of the molecule *capsaicin*, which is generated in the tissue that holds the seeds; it is also present in the internal membrane, and to a lesser extent the flesh. Alongside its use as a flavouring, its fiery nature means that capsaicin derived from chilies has a number of other roles, ranging from pain-relieving ointments to pepper sprays.

The heat of chilies used to be measured against the Scoville scale. In 1912 American chemist Wilbur Scoville developed his original test, in which panels of tasters were given sugar solutions containing a diluted pepper extract. The ratio

The lavender fields of Provence, France, are one of the most enduring of images of southern Europe. The fragrant plant is grown for the perfume trade, but it can still be found wild.

of dilution that was required in order for the chili's heat to be no longer detectable was then given as the measure of its potency.

The problem with the Scoville method was that it relied a great deal on subjectivity. So the heat of spices is now measured using a much more rigorous method – high-performance liquid chromatography.

The Mediterranean countries, meanwhile, possessed some of the richest herb stocks in Europe with oregano, bay – although originally from Asia Minor – hyssop, fennel, tarragon, lovage, marjoram, sage, rosemary and thyme. The Romans had done much to cultivate the art of growing and husbanding herbs in the region, and no legionnaire travelled without his personal herb collection.

A herb is a plant useful either by its leaf, flower, stem or root – as opposed to what the French call *les mauvaises herbes*, the weeds of the field – and they had uses beyond the mere pot herb. The bright blue-flowered hyssop flavoured salads and soups, but also made a useful strewing herb, spread out on earth floors where they acted like some medieval air freshener. Another herb valued for its scent, and still growing wild in the *maquis* of southern France, was lavender (from the Latin, *lavare*, 'to wash'), which was used to scent bath water. The inseparable twins oregano and marjoram were closely associated with the kitchen, yet Culpeper could identify no less than 20 parts of the body that benefited from marjoram's 'excellent remedy'. As for 'origane' – 'it groweth plentifully in the borders of corn fields' – there was 'scarce a better remedy growing for such as are troubled with sour humour in the stomach.'

Herbs and spices also played an important role in the monastic medicine cabinet. The Benedictine orders (Black Monks), the later Cistercians (White Monks) and Augustinians not only cultivated the cloistered *garth* (a neat lawn designed to 'nourish the eyes and preserve their vision') but also a physic garden of medicinal herbs and a small, locked poison garden where narcotics such as opium poppies, hemlock and mandrake were grown.

Herbs, they learned, should be harvested after the dew has dried, but before the heat of the day. They were best used fresh, but when they were to be stored, they were dried quickly and evenly on airing trays – in the modern household the microwave, set on low power for around three minutes, does the trick. Seeds were picked ripe, the stalks removed, and then stored in paper or cotton bags.

Herbs had countless uses. There were calming mint teas, antiseptic thyme – its essential oil, thymol, made a natural mouthwash – and pennyroyal to revive someone in a faint, St. John's Wort for depression and lettuce to promote sleep. In fact, the Romans used lettuce (*Lactuca sativa*) for a number of purposes,

CAPSICUM PEPPER

Name: Capsicum pepper
(*Capsicum annuum*)

What it's like: Most people are familiar with the edible bell pepper (*Capsicum annuum*), widely cultivated as a low-growing annual plant with dark green leaves and fruit that ripens from green to red, orange or yellow. *Capsicum annuum* is used in cooking, as a salad vegetable, and as the source of paprika, yet there are another 2,000 or 3,000 varieties including the chili peppers jalapeno, habanero, pimento, cayenne and serrano. The world-famous Tabasco sauce is obtained from the pepper *Capsicum frutescens*.

A relative of the tomato and potato – all members of the Solanaceae family – the sweet or chili pepper is native to the Americas, and was possibly named by Columbus when he discovered it in the Caribbean and associated it with the already known Asian spice black pepper.

This would have been due to capsaicin, the compound that creates the sensation of heat. Peppers are rated by their 'heat' or the amount of capsaicin they contain. Because of the painful sensation they can cause, capsaicans have been used as the basis of so called 'pepper sprays'. Ironically, they also have recognised medicinal qualities, being used to relieve pain and to relax arteries and reduce blood pressure.

Where it's grown: First domesticated in Mexico, capsicum peppers are now grown commercially throughout the tropical and subtropical regions including the United States, the Far East and East and West Africa.

including as a mild sedative, and even as late as the 1800s one Scottish doctor was selling his 'opium juice' made from lettuce.

Long before the monastic herbals were written, India and China had developed their own detailed herb guides. But from the monks' point of view there was one vital medicinal plant, famed for its laxative powers, and absent from their herbals: the Chinese drug *da huang*. The source of the drug was the rhubarb root (*Rheum palmatum*), but export restrictions imposed by the Chinese left the West frantically searching for a substitute until the 1750s when, to everyone's relief, it finally arrived.

Wild Food

Whenever there is shortage of food, people invariably fall back on their local supplies. Bush or wild foods naturally come into their own in times of crisis. They look nothing like the packaged foods of the supermarket shelves even though, in some instances, wild food is cleaner, fresher and healthier.

Our knowledge about the edibility of wild food has been gradually eroded as populations have drifted from village to town to city, and further from the fields that grow our foods. In earlier times several writers endeavoured to commit this native knowledge to print: Thomas Tusser in the 1500s listed 1,200 plants, many of them wild, that were useful to the housewife. They include marigolds, rocket, feverfew, poppies and ox-eye daisies. The ox-eye daisy roots were said by the 17th-century English writer and gardener John Evelyn to be eaten as a salad in Spain. Other field names for the common poppy, the 'headache' and 'poison' poppy for example, revived fears that the wild poppy (*Papaver rhoeas*) was a dangerous plant directly linked to the opium poppy (*Papaver somniferum*), yet the poppy seed heads yielded an abundance of grey seed ideal for sprinkling on top of any baked breads.

Bush food can also surprise. Dandelion leaves collected early in the season make a sharp-tasting salad – care should be taken with quantity for, as its old French and English folknames, *pissenlit* and piss-a-bed, suggest, the plant is an enuretic; horseradish root makes a hot sauce to accompany a joint of roast beef; a springtime crop of nettles can create a tasty soup. Some plants even yield several harvests on their own: elderflower can be dipped in batter and fried as fritters or used to make elderflower cordial, while its berries make wine and jelly. Elder pith is also used in the making of microscopy sections.

WILD STRAWBERRY

Name: Wild strawberry
(*Fragaria vesca*)

What it's like: The fruit is smaller and sweeter than the cultivated strawberry. The plant grows in scrub, woods and grassy places and is formed from rosettes of compound leaves, each with three toothed leaflets. The strawberry throws out many runners to create a mat of plants. The white flowers grow in clusters from a central stalk.

Wild strawberries were sold in Dutch markets in 1817, the fruit known as *Boskoeper* – since they were harvested from woods near Boskcoop: 'Children will bring them to you for a small reward', assured one French writer in 1669. In Turkey today hundreds of metric tons of wild fruit are harvested for export every year.

An Alpine version (*F. vesca*) grows in mountain regions, while the *hautbois* with its delicious tiny red fruits grows in European woodlands. The Virginian strawberry (*F. virginiana*), native to eastern parts of North America and found in woodlands and hedgerows, was known as *wattahimnerah* to the Native Americans who ground them together with Indian corn to make a bread. It was the Virginia strawberry that played an important role in the development of modern garden varieties.

Where it's grown: Throughout the Northern Hemisphere.

The most nutritious of all the wild foods, aside from mushrooms, are wild nuts. Gathering coconuts, pecans, sweet chestnuts, walnuts, almonds, hazels or the Australian macadamia often involves a race with the native wildlife, but there is usually enough to go round.

The sweet, or Spanish, chestnut (*Castanea sativa*), originally from southeast Europe and the Balkans, can not only be roasted, but also ground into flour, used to thicken soups, and for medicinal purposes. Walnuts (*Juglans* spp.) are found throughout the world and provide one of the richest and most expensive – unless the walnut is gathered free – salad dressings. Their shells have even been used as a metal cleaner and paint thickener. *Cordeauxia edulis*, or the ye'eb, which grows in the arid bush of Somalia and Ethiopia, has faced extinction because of over-grazing. Yet it yields a nutritious nut, a plant dye and foliage for animal fodder. Macadamia was long valued by Aboriginal people of Australia. It not only taste good raw, or rolled in chocolate, but has been associated with reductions in cholesterol.

Coming to appreciate wild field foods helps people engage with their surroundings and grasp the importance of conservation. But, while it can be hugely enjoyable to harvest your own crop of wild foods, common sense should be exercised: always use a good field guide, start with small portions and avoid any plants that might have been contaminated by passing traffic or sprays. Moreover, stripping a plant or pulling up a lone plant could jeopardise its species' future and many countries have introduced legislation to protect wild plants against being uprooted: if in doubt, look and leave alone. Remember that many edible wild plants can be bought as seeds and let loose in your own garden.

Field Fungi

Neither plant nor animal, fungi are among the strangest inhabitants of the field. Ranging from single-celled organisms to some of the largest living things on the planet, fungi can be found in a bewildering array of forms, but most commonly in the field as mushrooms, toadstools (the folkname for poisonous mushrooms) and truffles.

Fungi draw their food from decaying organic matter and living plants. Below ground lurks the *mycelium*, which, like the roots of a plant, spreads out to absorb the nutrients that sustain the fungi. The visible part, the mushroom, is merely the fruiting body, borne up to disperse spores for some new colony. They carry such a number of spores that if every one of the seven trillion contained in the average giant puffball survived, the resulting fungi would be 800 times heavier than the Earth. Aerial photographs have revealed fungi that are hundreds of years old, while Michigan's 'humongous fungus' is thought to be one of the world's largest and oldest organisms.

The fruiting bodies of mushroom and fungi come in an array of strange and wonderful shapes. Aside from the familiar 'umbrellas' there are orange cups, yellow brackets, stars and clubs, fungi shaped like soft sea coral, truffles like dark, pitted golf balls, and lewd, phallic fungi such as the common stinkhorn, named appropriately *Phallus impudicus* and renowned for its rank smell.

Although some fungi are harmful – dry rot, for example, feeds on house timbers – others have a history of helping human life along. There are the fungi that flavour gorgonzola and most blue cheeses; others provide enzymes for washing powders; still others play a medicinal role, *Penicillium*, for example, or

Poisonous fungi published in the German *Meyers Konversations-Lexikon*, in 1897. The fairytale white-spotted red toadstool at bottom middle is called the fly agaric (*Amanita muscaria*).

supply natural dyes – the red-gilled web-cap (*Cortinarius semisanguineus*) is the source of a brilliant red dye, while the green-stain cup fungus (*Chlorociboria aeruginosa*) colours its host wood bright blue-green.

To many people, mushrooms and fungi represent the most flavoursome of the wild foods. Armed with a foldaway knife and open basket – mushrooms bruise easily and they need air space when collected – the mushroom collector, having found his or her prey, makes a note of its surroundings, and these days takes a digital photo, before picking the fungi. Only young, but not too young, and fresh fungi are picked, the stem twisted until it breaks free, or severed with the knife – tearing a fungus can disturb the mycelium underground and inhibit growth of future fruiting bodies.

In the summer fields, the fungi hunter might be fortunate enough to come across a strange, gleaming white globe nestling like a new football in the grass. The giant puffball (*Calvatia gigantea*, loosely translated as 'giant bald head') is a wonder to look at and a treat to eat. The giant puffball is reputed to grow up to the size of a small sheep, and yields steak after steak of creamy fungus perfect when fried in the field over a camping stove, dressed with a dash of pepper and lemon, or dipped in beaten egg and breadcrumbs. Mature puffballs have also been used for stanching blood flow, for smoking bees and as kindling.

Once in the kitchen the fungi hunter will check his or her finds with an expert or a detailed field guide before cooking or preserving them. This is especially important because poisonous and edible fungi can be easily confused.

Wild mushrooms can be sautéed, pickled in olive oil or vinegar, or made into *duxelles*, sautéed with chopped onions, salt and pepper in a little butter before being frozen. They can also be dried in an oven, a process that improves the flavour of some fungi such as the common morel (*Morchella esculenta*).

Foremost among the fungi treasures is the truffle, which has acquired an almost legendary status, and is best consumed raw; for example, as fine shavings scattered over lightly scrambled eggs. Unlike parasol mushrooms, the truffle bears tuber-like fruit bodies below ground. The summer truffle (*T. aestivum*) grows across Europe, including southern Scandinavia; the highly prized white truffle (*T. magnatum*) hides beside the roots of oaks, poplars and willows in the Piedmont region of northwest Italy; the royal truffle, the Périgord (*T. melansporum*), grows not only in this region of France, but also in the southern départements and in Italy and Spain, in oak and hazel woods. Young trees have been inoculated with truffle spores to provide a harvest after ten years or so, and the truffles are found by specially trained dogs and pigs.

In summer and early autumn one of the deadliest of the gilled fungi breaks through the surface. The ominously named death cap (*Amanita phalloides*) metamorphoses from a green-capped young fruit body to a parasol-shaped mushroom with pale, free gills, a greenish cap and a prominent white *volva*, the base of the plant. The destroying angel (*A. virosa*) is equally poisonous and can easily be confused with edible fungi.

However, although the *Amanita* genus includes some of the most poisonous mushrooms, not all are potential killers. Fly agaric (*A. muscaria*), the classic fairy-tale toadstool, is poisonous, yet the tawny grisette (*A. fulva*) is edible when well cooked, while Caesar's mushroom (*A. caesarea*) makes for a great meal.

Potent Plants

As is the case with fungi, the plants of the field hold some particularly unpleasant surprises in store for the unwary. Relatively small doses of some plants, for example, yew (*Taxus baccata*) and the roots of cowbane (*Cicuta virosa*), or water hemlock as it is also known, can have an immediate and fatal effect. Others such as bracken (*Pteridium aquilinum*) can be consumed in larger quantities over a long period before their poisonous effects become apparent. The picture is confused further by the fact that certain plants are poisonous to specific animals, but will leave others unaffected; acorns, for example, will poison a cow, but fatten a pig.

Poisonous plants can, however, benefit humankind. Foxglove (*Digitalis purpurea*), despite its natural toxicity, has long been recognised as a treatment for heart conditions; while, following plant screening by the World Health Organisation in the 1970s, oil from cotton plant seeds was identified as a source of the male contraceptive, gossypol, which also has anti-malarial properties. The leaves of the coca plant (*Erythroxylum coca*), grown on the mountain terraces of the Andes, are still used in that area and nearby Peru by country people coping with the hardships of a labouring life on an inadequate diet. Its active ingredient, the alkaloid cocaine, was identified in the 1840s, and has since been exploited as the recreational drug cocaine, but also in medicine. Cocaine is no longer used in medicine these days, but synthetics such as lignocaine, benzocaine and procaine (trade name Novocain) are used as substitutes.

Knowledge of poisonous plants has been passed down the generations, mostly by word of mouth but increasingly in written form. The Incas, for example, set down much of their knowledge in pictographs, but most were destroyed by their Spanish conquerors. In 60 C.E. Dioscorides, an army surgeon, completed his *De Materia Medica*, a work describing more than 600 plants. It would serve as the leading herbal in Europe for the next 16 centuries. A German botanist, J. F. Gmelin, produced his own guide in 1775, while in 1804 a French-man, M. J. B. Ortila, set about methodically poisoning dogs to come up with his own list. When Nicholas Culpeper published his own *Complete Herbal* in 1653, he noted the virtues, and the malevolences, of many field plants. Of bryony he warned: 'They are furious martial plants: the roots ... purge the belly with great violence, troubling the stomach, and burning the liver.' Culpeper was a campaign-ing herbalist: dog's mercury, for example, he condemned as 'a rank, poisonous plant. There is not a more fatal plant, native of our country [Britain] than this.' Other writers, he wrote, have warned of its dangers 'in Latin, a language not likely to inform those who stand most in need of this caution. This is one of the reasons for compiling this work.'

Although a few disgruntled husbands and wives may have dipped into nature's pharmacopeia to dispose of a tiresome partner, it was the farmer, concerned for his stock, who took the closest interest. The toxicity of some plants lay undetected for centuries; for instance, the ill-effects of ragwort (*Senecio jacobaea*) was not established until 1906 when Canadian scientists realised that Pictou disease was caused by ragwort or what the Scots called 'stinking willy'. Ragwort was also behind the incidence of South Africa's Molteno cattle disease. Although its more common victims were farm animals, especially horses, stinking willy was said to have been taken by country women to induce abortion, often with fatal consequences. Poisonous plants still kill animals: they took their toll of 16 per cent of animals in America in the 1990s.

The potential toxicity of certain plants contains some surprises: oleander, daffodil bulbs, holly, cuckoo-pint flower and fruits, comfrey (*Symphytum officinale*), white bryony, bindweed, lupin, monkshood, mistletoe, meadow saffron and

'They [bryony] are furious martial plants: the roots ... Purge the belly with great violence, troubling the stomach, and burning the liver.'

Nicholas Culpeper, *Complete Herbal*, 1653

COFFEE

Name: Coffee
(*Coffea arabica*)

What it's like: *Coffea arabica* is an Ethiopian and Yemenese species of coffee also called the 'coffee shrub of Arabia'. Coffee beans, roasted, ground and brewed with hot water, are drunk by a third of the world's population, making coffee the single most valuable farm export of the tropics.

Coffee trees, which are productive for around 30 years, are pruned to keep the crop within the range of the coffee pickers. The sweet-smelling white flowers produce a green berry that ripens to a red colour, and each contains two – sometimes one – seeds (or beans).

For harvesting the berries are opened, the beans fermented briefly in water and then sun-dried, leaving the bean in its inner skin. It is exported in this form as 'mild' coffee – mild means best quality. A 'hard' or lower-quality coffee is produced by sun-drying the berries, and milling them to remove the inner skin.

Where it's grown: Mostly in the Americas, especially Brazil and Colombia. There is also Jamaican Blue Mountain, Costa Rican and Salvadoran coffee.

The incidence of leaf diseases makes growing difficult in the lowland areas of other parts of the world, but the highland coffees of Kenya and India enjoy a good reputation.

hemlock. One of nature's more infamous poisons, it is thought that it was hemlock (*Conium maculatum*) that accounted for the death of the Athenian philosopher, Socrates, in 399 B.C.E. Found guilty of, among other things, 'refusing to recognise the gods recognised by the state', the 70-year-old was sentenced to death by drinking the 'state poison'. But it is recorded that he took his potion with stoicism. Paralyzing the central nervous system, hemlock causes a slow death. As his limbs grew cold and the poison spread towards his heart Socrates remembered a debt, 'Crito, we owe a cock to Asclepius. Do pay it. Don't forget', he told his friend. And died.

Culpeper offered advice to anyone who took hemlock in error, 'The strongest and best wine they can procure.' And 'If wine cannot be instantly had, Pliny adviseth to take a good draught of strong vinegar, which he affirms to be a sovereign remedy.'

Some field plants started out with the promise of pleasure, but turned into a source of pain. When *Nicotiana tabacum*, the tobacco plant, was brought to Europe from the Americas by Francis Drake it was hailed by Culpeper as a good medicine for rheumatic pains. Made into an ointment 'with hog's lard it is good for the piles when they get painful and are inflamed.' The powdered leaves, he wrote, were a powerful insecticide, inhibited the appetite – making it 'useful to the more gross' – it was a 'great expeller of phlegm', had the power to revive someone who had apparently drowned, and could kill a cat with a single drop.

The pre-Columbian people used tobacco for ceremonial purposes. By the 16th century the Portuguese were cultivating it commercially in Brazil. Monardes, a doctor from Seville, Spain, commended it as a curative. The practice of 'drinking' the smoke, as one commentator put it, swept across Europe, and it was even claimed to be a cure for cancer. Tobacco became so profitable that it earned fortunes in taxes: in some societies it even displaced hard cash as a currency. In wartime troops were issued with cigarettes along with their ammunition to calm their nerves – nicotine, the active ingredient, tranquillises the nervous system. Today it generates huge profits, but is seriously damaging to health.

Other plants caused problems of their own. Hemp was known to the Chinese for over 4,000 years and has been used to make paper, rope, food and fuel. It requires no pesticides and provides a biodegradable material for packaging.

Tea plantations in Indonesia were founded by Dutch colonists during the 19th century. Today the country produces around 5 per cent of the world's tea crop.

But one strain of hemp (*Cannabis sativa*) was smoked as *hashish* (from the Persian *ashishin*, which has given us two words: hashish and assassin). Another narcotic was extracted from the peyote, a Mexican cactus (*Lophophora williamsii*) and the preferred drug of the shaman seeking to commune with the spirit world.

Three other plants, however, have been adopted the world over because of a particular active ingredient, caffeine: cocoa – not to be confused with coca, the source of cocaine – tea and coffee. Cocoa (*Theobromo cacao*) grows on a small tree originally in the American tropics, but now mostly in West Africa. Curiously, the flower grows from the main trunk, producing pods of beans that are scooped out and fermented, often in heaps covered with banana leaves. The beans contain 50 to 57 per cent cocoa butter that is used to make chocolate, a food that contains a small amount of caffeine and a related alkaloid, theobromine.

Tea comes from the leaves of the tea tree (*Camellia sinensis*), which once grew wild from India to China. The best-quality tea is picked from the terminal bud and the two lower leaves. These are withered, rolled, fermented, dried and graded, a process that turns the leaves black. In the Far East the demand is higher for green tea, where the leaves are gently heated at an early stage to inhibit fermentation. China is the largest tea-growing country – although the Chinese drink most of what they grow – followed by India and Sri Lanka, while Russia, Britain and Australia are the biggest importers of tea.

Plant Dyes

Composing their colours a century ago, country people extracted pigments from local materials, from chalk and soured milk, pig and ox blood, and plants on the field margins. At dyeing time women fetched their bramble baskets and filled them with lichens, carrageen moss, heather, ragwort, iris, madder and woad.

Hillside heathers died wool yellow; madder produced a pale red, as did the roots of the dandelion; gorse and ragwort gave shades of brown, while woad created a deep blue. Greens were more difficult to produce – many considered the colour unlucky – while black, made from yellow flag iris with chips of oak and urine added, was used to colour clothes. In addition, there were lavender hues from elderberries, purple tones from blackberries, and various shades of orange from bloodroot, sassafras leaves, onion skins and lichens.

Madder (*Rubia tinctoria*) and woad (*Isatis tinctoria*) were two of the most important plants. In 1660, a thousand people were employed at one madder plantation by the Thames near London. The Dutch were masters at growing madder, and other countries sent farmers to Zeeland to learn the art of its cultivation. Meanwhile, the art of turning woad into the blue dye that coloured the cheap working clothes of the field labourers was mastered by French dyers – although the putrid smell of processing woad made the dyers themselves unpopular. Grown in Britain it was known as *glasto*, the town of Glastonbury, in Somerset, being the place 'where woad grows'.

But there was another plant, equally smelly in its preparation, that would supplant woad: indigo (*Indigofera tinctoria*). Used extensively in West Africa and Asia, indigo, or *nil* in Hindi and Bengali, was extracted by soaking the leaves of the plant in urine and leaving them to ferment. The dyed cloth smelled rank when it first came out of the pot.

Natural dyes were replaced gradually by chemical dyes, heralded by the arrival of Prussian blue – made from alum and animal bones – in the 18th century. Country dyeing, however, continued. After all, the materials were free, and the processes simple. Muslins, wools, cottons and silks dyed easily provided the flowers were picked in full bloom, the berries used when they were ripe, and the nuts when mature. The plant materials were chopped up, boiled in twice the quantity of water, and then simmered for an hour or so. Meanwhile the cloth was soaked in a fixative – salt-based for berry dyes, vinegar-based for plants – before being dipped, still wet, into the dye bath. If necessary they were left to soak overnight to achieve deeper, stronger colours.

Whenever conflict threatened the import of a dye, the dyers turned back to their own fields; nettles, for example, were used as a camouflage dye in the Second World War, while the young tips of cow parsley produced a yellow-green dye used in the making of Harris Tweed. Even now dye plants are enjoying a revival as the quest for more sustainable sources of dyes makes an impact.

❧

Chapter Eight

FIELD
FOLKLORE

Fields create both a barrier and a link between the true wilderness and where we live. Every region has its own collection of tales and folklore that revolves around the field. Moreover, such folk tales and folk art have informed every sphere of artistic endeavour, from music and song to literature and fine art.

The Field Scene

A simple embroidery is laid out among other tourist souvenirs – zebu-horn dominoes and toys cut from old sardine cans – on a market stall near Nosy Be, in northern Madagascar. The needlework depicts, beneath a blue sky and a beaming sun, fishermen in *pirogues* (dug-out canoes), *pousse-pousses* (rickshaws), bush taxis or *taxis-brousse*, women bearing baskets on their heads, and a *charette* (wooden cart) of hay pulled by a zebu. All are surrounded by a wash of hump-backed grain fields and paddies.

The iconic field can be purchased for a few *ariary* at a street-side market in Madagascar, or for thousands of dollars in the fine-art auction houses of Sydney or Seattle. For the more industrialised and removed from the land a society becomes, the more its urban citizens yearn for the pastoral pleasures they associate with the field. Summer fields suggest the simple life: bird song and bumble bees, flowers and sunshine – in short, pure pastoralism.

In its literal sense, pastoralism means managing livestock in a pasture. Pastoral tribes, such as the Maasai of East Africa, grazed their sheep, goats or cattle in those places where arable crops could not be grown. In its figurative sense – for example, Beethoven's 1808 'Pastoral' symphony – the pastoral evoked the rural idyll. Beethoven wrote the Pastoral to reflect the unhurried pace of country life. *Mañana* (tomorrow), say the Spanish Castillians; *kamosos* (tomorrow), say the Motswana; *mora, mora* (slowly, slowly), say the Malagasy.

The pastoral had a strong appeal for both the Greeks and Romans. The poet Theocritus, credited with creating ancient Greek *bucolic* poetry (from the Greek for 'cowherd') in the third century B.C.E., set many of his pastoral idylls in the

Rural idylls such as this scene in Sussex, England, have inspired the movement of pastoralism, which idealises the relationship between humankind and nature, as embodied by the field.

romantic, rural surroundings of his island home. The classical Roman poet Publius Vergilius Maro (70–19 B.C.E.), better known as Virgil and himself a farmer's son, placed his own pastoral *Eclogues* in a rustic paradise, Arcadia, and peopled it with pretty shepherd boys. Artifacts from Theocritus's and Virgil's time, friezes of bucolic cherubs gathering the grape harvest or silver figurines of shepherds and shepherdesses, illustrate the Greek and Roman passion for the pastoral. Yet similar scenes depicting village markets, ploughmen in the field or milkmaids in their dairies were to be found throughout the ancient world, painted on palace and manor walls in India, Japan, Korea and China.

Two thousand years on, such idealised scenes of country life were still being trafficked. In an issue of *Cassell's Family Magazine* from the late 1890s, a group of smiling women were pictured cheerfully raking the turned hay ready to be pitch-forked on to the haywain's wagon. The illustration was accompanied by the caption: 'As we hover round the hay, Airy throngs of sweetest songs, Fragrant as roses, light as foam.'

'Corny' scenes like these were designed to remind city folk from New England to New Zealand of a golden age when honest families worked the fields in a kind of hazy arcadia. In the West the popularity of the pastoral scene was heightened by the Industrial Revolution. When the Spinning Jenny industrialised the work of the cottage weavers, the labouring families were forced to move into the mill towns and developed a longing for their half-remembered pastoral past. In later years, and especially when war or conquest threatened, this sentimental love of the land continued to tug at people's hearts. When the poet Rupert Brooke died on a hospital ship in the Aegean in 1915 before he could be truly exposed to the horrors of the First World War, he had already penned 'The Soldier' (1914): 'If I should die, think only this of me: That there's some corner of a foreign field; That is for ever England.' The field had developed a literary currency all of its own.

The Field in Literature

There are plenty of children's tales and folk stories that may not represent the highest of literary aspirations, but nevertheless reflect the crucial place of the field. Such tales remind us of the days 'When daisies pied and violets blue, And lady-smocks all silver-white, And cuckoo-buds of yellow hue, Do paint the meadows with delight,' as Shakespeare put it in *Love's Labour's Lost*.

Before the Industrial Revolution, country commentators celebrated the pastoral; afterwards they mourned its passing. Riding the American prairies, William Cullen Bryant recalled 'A race … that long passed away' in 'The Prairies' (1832). 'These ample fields, Nourished their harvests, here their herds were fed; When haply by their stalls the bison lowed, And bowed his maned shoulder to the yoke. All day this desert murmured with their toils, Til twilight blushed.'

Alfred, Lord Tennyson also dwelt on the transient nature of life in the field when he wrote 'Tithonus' (1860): 'The woods decay, the woods decay and fall; The vapours weep their burthen to the ground; Man comes and tills the field and lies beneath.'

The poets who did not have to toil in the field could afford to romanticise the pastoral delights of country life. In Renaissance Europe they began to mimic Virgil. The poets included the Italian Petrarch and England's Edmund Spenser who, in the 16th century, went on to compose the acclaimed *Fairy Queene*. Spenser had already translated other European pastoral poets such as Clément Marot when he composed *The Shepherd's Calendar* in 1597: 'Bring hither the pink and purple columbine, With Gillyflowers …, Strew me the ground with Daffadowndillies, And Cowslips, and Kingcups, and loved Lilies.'

The *Calendar*, a series of eclogues or pastoral poems, borrowed its title from a farmers' almanac, *The Kalender and Compost of Shepherds*, published the previous century. In writing his *Calendar* Spenser was following the advice of his peers who believed that young poets, lacking the necessary life experiences on which to versify, should draw on their imaginings of life in the lyrical field. (Ironically, the hard realities of rural life were brought home to Spenser 18 years later when disaffected land workers burned down his castle in Ireland.)

In the centuries that followed, more pastoral works would be published including John Milton's *Lycidas* (1637); John Gay's *The Shepherd's Week*, a droll

'When daisies pied and violets blue,
And lady-smocks all silver-white,
And cuckoo-buds of yellow hue,
Do paint the meadows with delight'

William Shakespeare, *Love's Labour's Lost*, c. 1598

account of country characters in his home county, Devon; and Alexander Pope's *Pastorals* (1709), a work that would be parodied by the down-to-earth George Crabbe. 'I grant indeed that fields and flocks have charms, For him that gazes or for him that farms,' wrote Crabbe in *The Village* (1783). Later he would remind his readers of the old adage that a happy farmer was as rare as a dead donkey, 'Our farmers round, well pleased with constant gain, Like other farmers, flourish and complain' (*The Parish Register*, 1807).

While coffee-house poets continued to eulogise about life in the field, others endeavoured to record the realities. John Clare, himself the son of a farm labourer, railed against the English Enclosure Acts (see page 49), while another farm labourer's son, William Cobbett, after riding through England, concluded: 'It is to blaspheme God to suppose that he created men to be miserable, to hunger, thirst, and perish with cold, in the midst of that abundance which is the fruit of their own labour' (*Cottage Economy*, 1821).

The visionary artist and poet William Blake was another commentator with a desire for social justice for the rural poor. 'He who shall hurt the little wren; Shall never be loved by men. He who the ox to wrath has moved, Shall never be by woman loved' (*Auguries of Innocence*, 1803), wrote the man who had been deeply influenced by the French and American revolutions. Blake saw not the absurd cavorting of nymphs and shepherds, but its enduring nature: 'The sword sung on the barren heath; The sickle in the fruitful field: The sword he sung a song of death; But could not make the sickle yield.' (*Gnomic Verses*, XIV).

Blake the artist was better known than Blake the poet, although his work would be rediscovered by the Pre-Raphaelites who, through men like William Morris, attacked the industrial age and celebrated instead the handcrafts that the machine age made redundant. 'Have nothing in your houses that you do not know to be useful, or believe to be beautiful,' wrote Morris with an eye, perhaps, on the simple wood, leather and iron tools of the field that hung on the farmhouse walls. (When Morris died in 1896 his plain oak coffin was borne to the grave-yard on a decorated farm wagon.)

Eighteen years later it was the field of battle rather than the farm field that had a particular resonance. Wilfred Owen – 'My subject is War, and the pity of War' – was killed in France a week before the end of the First World War. Earlier he wrote of a fallen comrade in his poem 'Futility': 'Move him into the sun – Gently its touch awoke him once, At home, whispering of fields unsown.'

Few writers focused exclusively on the field, but one notable exception was the Irish playwright John B. Keane whose *The Field*, subsequently made into a film, centred on the farmer 'Bull' McCabe and his passion for the land he rented. Another exception was a story written by the French novelist Marcel Pagnol of a bitter family feud that arose around a spring-fed field high in the Provençal hills of southern France. The subsequent films, *Jean de Florette* and *Manon des Sources* (1986), drew wide acclaim.

Field Art

High in the hills of Crete, the patronne of a roadside café has decorated her walls with country scenes: a cutting from a local newspaper of a prize Simmental bull, a postcard of the surrounding mountains under snow, and, incongruously, a reproduction of *The Hay Wain* by the English painter John Constable. *The Hay Wain* can be found, cut from chocolate-box covers or turned into jigsaw puzzles, in homes from Canberra to Canterbury. The Suffolk borders scene looks the picture of pastoral peace with its skyline of elms – the trees would all be felled in the 1970s when Dutch elm disease struck Britain – and its wagoner and his cart resting in the millstream beside a rambling farmhouse.

Constable was recording the field as artists had done for centuries: although Roman life was centred on its cities, most villa owners earned their *denarii* from their grapes and grain, their cattle and sheep, a fact borne out by the wall paintings, mosaics and bronzes that celebrated rural life. Half a world away, China and Japan similarly celebrated the field in their decorative arts: one wall painting, found in Jiayuguan, China, of an animated farmer riding his ox-driven plough, could be dated back to 100 B.C.E. More common, though, were scenes from the Japanese *tanbo* or paddy field, filled with wading workers under their straw capes and conical hats, and Chinese peasants pictured sheltering from the sun beneath their *dou li* straw hats, picking leaves in the tea plantations.

In Europe too the landscape painters diligently recorded the field. In 17th-century Holland, the Dutch painters, surrounded by some of Europe's most advanced agricultural fieldscapes, included Jacob Van Ruisdael, who captured the sun sweeping across the flatlands of Antwerp and floodlighting a cornfield in *An Extensive Landscape with Ruins*. In *The Avenue at Middelharnis* (1689), Meijndert Hobbema pictured water-filled ditches and deep green pastures with, in one corner of the painting, a market gardener pruning trees in a little nursery: increasingly artists were portraying not just the fieldscape, but those who farmed it.

Among them were the animal portraitists. When in the 18th century Western agriculture expanded to meet the demands of its growing population, farm artists were paid to portray the animal breeders with their prize bulls, stallions, mares, hogs and ewes, an idea that has been repeated in the 21st century by the photographer Yann Arthus-Bertrand.

One of the most iconic images of field work is Jean-François Millet's *The Gleaners* (1857), depicting three women collecting fallen grain. Millet's series of scenes of peasants at work including *The Sower* and *The Angelus* – his work influenced Vincent van Gogh and Claude Monet – were executed around the time when some of his fellow artists were earning their money from the French seed firm, Vilmorin. Philippe-Victoire de Vilmorin, responsible for introducing the field beetroot and rutabaga, or swede, to France, was also an ingenious publicist. When colour printing appeared in the second half of the 1800s, he paid the Paris watercolourists to lavishly illustrate the company's catalogues and seed packets. Postcard prints of their work are still sold on the streets of Paris.

In the United States, meanwhile, painters like William Sydney Mount and Eastman Johnson were at work in the field. Like Mount, Johnson dealt with the business of field slaves – *Life in the South, Old Kentucky Home* (1859) – while his

The Hay Wain by John Constable, finished in1821, is one of Britain's best-loved paintings. It depicts a hay wagon near Flatford Mill on the River Stour in Suffolk, England.

crisp *Cranberry Harvest, Nantucket Island* (1880), which depicted whole families on their hands and knees in the berry fields, celebrated the theme that occupied artists, naive and sophisticated, from the beginning of time: while the art world passed from one stylistic movement to the next, the harvest endured. And always there was an artist to record it.

The Viennese painter Gustav Klimt was well known for his sensuous paintings. He seemed to sensualise the field itself with the *Apfelbaum* (*Apple Tree*) where a tree, dimpled with ripe fruit, stood knee-deep in a flowering meadow. In his earlier *Field of Poppies* (1907) there were echoes of the flowering French meadows of the Impressionist Claude Monet's iconic *The Poppy Field at Argenteuil* (1873), where two women walk their children through a blossoming field. Fauvism bridged the world of the post-Impressionists and Cubism, and when the Fauvist French artist Raoul Dufy turned his attention to the harvest in *Le Champ de blé* (*The Wheatfield*), he painted the three horses that drew the mechanical reaper through a yellow field of standing corn bright blue and red – and added a mysterious white horse emerging from the uncut corn.

One year on, the American regionalist Grant Wood presaged the hay harvest with the painting that made him into a national figure, his stylised *American Gothic* (1930), depicting a stonefaced farmer in his workmen's bib and brace, holding a pitchfork, beside his worried-looking wife – the models were actually the artist's sister and his dentist.

By now, however, American artists such as Alexandre Hogue (*Drouth Stricken Area*, 1934 and *The Crucified Land*, 1939) and Jerry Bywaters (*On the Ranch*, 1941) were coming to terms, pictorially, with the American Dust Bowl and the failed harvests brought on by land erosion. The writer James Agee and photographer Walker Evans were also recording the results of the eight-year-long drought in the southern plains where many of the 'Okies' (from Oklahoma) gave up and became migrant labourers, making their way to states like California where there was never enough work. John Steinbeck's *Of Mice and Men* (1937) and *The Grapes of Wrath* (1939) exposed some of their hardships, but it was Dorothea Lange who produced one of the most powerful images of the 1930s with her photograph of Florence Owens Thompson sheltering with her children in a lean-to tent, having sold the tires from her car to buy food. *Migrant Mother*, as the picture became known, was an image that would haunt the world.

Less than a decade later, on the other side of the Atlantic, there was a conscious return to pastoralism when artists like Frank Newbould produced stylised poster prints of the British harvest scene, pictures that were used by

Second World War propagandists to evoke a land worth fighting for. But in the post-war years a new realism emerged. Andrew Wyeth's *Christina's World*, a painting that was to become one of the best-known images of American 20th-century art, portrayed a young woman lying in a field and looking longingly at a distant farmhouse – in truth the subject, Christina Olson, was disabled and physically incapable of climbing up to the house. Other works by Wyeth such as *Tenant Farmer* (1961), in which a dead deer hangs from a bare tree behind the farmhouse, finally laid to rest the lie of pastoralism.

It seemed a far cry from Constable's *Hay Wain*. Yet the two paintings were as honest as each other in their depictions of country life. Constable's scene was painted when northern Europe was powering a great agricultural revolution. *The Hay Wain* is not a peaceful image: with grain yields soaring, the mill, attached to the cottage in the background, was gearing up for the coming harvest as men mow the hay on the far side of the river. The wagoner, meanwhile, had probably driven his cart into the stream to swell its wooden wheels against their new iron bindings. There was work to be done in the fields.

Field Songs

If it were somehow possible to push a play-back button on the field, extraordinary sounds would emerge. Cotton fields would thump out the rhythms of long-dead slaves pacing their picking to their music. Paddy fields would resonate with the high-pitched songs of the women workers. Tiny fields of fava beans and lentils in Mali would resonate to the ululations of African women. Alpine meadows would ring with the forgotten yodels of shepherds.

Songs revolved around just about any field work: hewing, hauling, ploughing, reaping, spinning, weaving, making ropes in Greece and drawing water in North Africa. The waulking song was practised by Hebridean women as they worked on the shrinking and fulling of hand-woven textiles. Led by one singer, the song lines were repeated, with a chorus, by the other women.

The yodel is one of the strangest field sounds. Popularised in the 19th century by cowboy songs such as *The Old Chisholm Trail*, sung by the cattle herders as they

The trauma of the American Dust Bowl in the 1930s gave birth to such literary classics as John Steinbeck's *Grapes of Wrath* and *Of Mice and Men*.

trailed from Texas to Kansas, the music was picked up by the makers of Hollywood westerns who made yodelling movie stars of men like Tom Mix and Tex Ritter. Yodel, from the German *jodeln* (what the French called *chanter à la manière Tyrolienne*, singing in the Tyrolean way), meant to call, cry or sing with a distinctive falsetto sound, and it had been taken to America by European migrants.

The sound of the falsetto cry was traditionally used by people to keep in touch with each other across the fields. The old cries were gradually incorporated into different singing styles still heard in places like Ethiopia, Burundi, Gabon, Papua New Guinea, Brazil and the Solomon Islands.

Field songs evolved into the folk music of different nations. The Qingpu field songs, native to Shanghai in China, were based on the Wuyue culture, and were sung in the rice fields. As well as being sung by the rice workers themselves, they were performed by semi-professionals who, in their childhood, learned to master the strange high and low octaves and improvise the words of songs that could run to thousands of lines. At busy times of the year the singing masters would direct the labourers in the rice fields, singing their songs and beating a rhythm out on a drum or gong.

Nursery songs often relate to the field. There was 'Old MacDonald Had a Farm' and patting rhymes like 'To market, to market, to buy a fat pig; home again, home again, jigadee jig.' One Russian song warned children to behave for 'The horned goat is coming: To those who don't eat porridge; To those who don't drink milk; To those children she will go; Butt! Butt! Butt!'

Blowing the dandelion clock might be accompanied by the chant: 'Field horses, field horses, what's the time of day? One o'clock [one breath] two o'clock [another breath] three [big breath].' In another variation it was 'Bell horse, bell horse', a reference to the tradition of hanging bells from the leading packhorse.

'We plough the fields and scatter
The good seed on the land,
But it is fed and watered
By God's almighty hand'

Matthias Claudius, 'We Plough the Fields and Scatter', c. 1775

Then there was a virtual chorus of songs dedicated to the farmyard hen: 'Hickety, pickety, my black hen; She lays eggs for gentlemen' and 'Good morning, Mrs. Hen; How many chickens have you got? Madam, I've got ten.'

Neither was the pig – 'Tom, Tom, the piper's son, Stole a pig and away did run' – the cow – 'Hey diddle diddle, the cat and the fiddle, The cow jumped over the moon' – nor the sheep – 'Little Boy Blue come blow up your horn, The sheep's in the meadow, the cow's in the corn' – left out. There were skipping songs, clapping songs and stepping songs, for rhythm came before tune or harmony. 'When you worked the seed fiddle you had to sing a song or whistle a tune to get the rhythm as you walked along,' recalled one labourer.

Cotton plantations were renowned, not only for their rhythmic songs, but for their field hollers: 'Sun up, sun down, picking that cotton, no more auction block for me.' The field holler, also sung by mule skinners and field hands in the rice and sugar plantations, was called by one singer, urged on by their workmates, and echoed by the others. Field hollering was influenced by, and possibly gave rise to, blues music just as American tap dancing owed its origins to the cotton slaves. When the pickers lacked a drum – because it had been taken from them by the plantation manager – the slaves took up the rhythm with their feet.

Field songs changed with the seasons. The German poet Matthias Claudius's sturdy harvest hymn 'Wir pflügen und wir streuen' (translated into English as: 'We plough the fields and scatter, The good seed on the land') is traditionally belted out in the autumn; while the rainy season in Africa is greeted with gratitude: 'Fall rain, fall rain: beautiful rain' sang South Africa's Ladysmith Black Mambazo. A traditional Irish blessing song wished 'the sun shine warm upon your face, the rains fall soft upon your fields.'

Migrant workers carried their field songs with them wherever they went. Irish labourers who travelled to Australia took along their songs, elaborating on them in the new country. One such hand-me-down was the shearer's song: 'Out on the board the old shearer stands; Grasping his shears in his thin bony hands; Fixed is his gaze on a bare-bellied yoe; Glory if he gets her, won't he make the ringer go. Click go the shears boys, click, click, click; Wide is his blow and his hands move quick; The ringer looks around and is beaten by a blow; And curses the old snagger with the bare-bellied yoe.'

Field songs are still being sung and written. One Scottish songwriter, Ali Burns, composed her song 'Fenland' for a Norwich, England, choir, Big Sky. 'Ghosts cling to dust that blows in four directions across the sky on the wind that steals our soil; One hundred thousand acres three times drained fenland cuts to reach the sea. And the sea is a hungry one and it takes its fill in quiet ways over the years as the fenland sighs the coastline grows; Down from the deep in the heart of the fen. Down from the deep a long boat rises.'

The songwriter explained: 'The "dust that blows in four directions" represents over-fertilisation and the creation of a soil that has lost its structure and is turning back to dust. "The sea is a hungry one" is about the constant movement of the coastline caused by drainage and sea-erosion.' Her first line, 'Ghosts cling to dust,' came from stories about how, as drainage caused land levels to sink, the old ghosts that once walked on the ground now appeared up in the air.

Field Legends

Legends of the field are legion and global. Africa, with more than 2,000 different languages, is home to numerous field tales; for example, that of the hare who was too lazy to plough his own field, so fooled an elephant into dragging his chains to save himself the trouble.

For the Bedouin many myths surrounded the famous Arab horse. One concerned the 'flea-bitten' grey with a distinctive red shoulder mark. She was originally a grey mare who had carried the Prophet Mohammed into battle. When he was wounded in the fight, the loyal horse brought her master home, his blood staining her coat with the tell-tale mark. Elsewhere, the blood stain has been a frequent theme: from poppies, said to have been marked by the blood of Christ, to the passion flower whose anthers represented Christ's wounds.

The cornflower – also known as the bluecap, bluet or hurtsickle because it blunted the mower's scythe – was, according to Russian legend, a young man called Basilek, who was lured into the corn field by a nymph, Russalka, and turned into a cornflower. Corn spirits are common the world over and can be seen, so they say, moving through the fields on ripples of wind. At harvest time the spirits retreat before the reapers' blades until finally they hide, trapped in the last stand of corn.

A little corn dolly, knot, kern baby or mell doll – depending on where you came from – was fashioned from the last harvest sheaf to keep the corn spirits safe for the following spring. Alternatively the harvester bound the last sheaf into a figure that represented the spirit – variously known in Germany as the menacing bullkaters, haferboks, kornwolves or roggerhunds – and carefully preserved it until the next year's sowing. In Estonia, a country that has preserved its folklore longer than its more agriculturally developed neighbours, the *Metsik*, a straw man or woman, was placed on a tree or fence to keep the cattle safe from wild animals and promote fertility in the field. Then there was the *Tonn* (possibly derived from St. Anthony), a cloth and wax doll kept in the bushel basket in the granary and presented with an offering of the first of any fruit harvest.

For the Romans, Ceres was the goddess of the harvest while in Greece it was Demeter who had bestowed the gift of wheat on mankind. 'Who sows wheat, sows God', so they said.

In Scotland the corn spirit was the Old Wife; in Brittany, France, the Mother Sheaf; in parts of Germany, the Harvest Mother, to be borne home on the last wagon and ritually watered – or soaked – on the way; the Danes had their Rye Woman and Old Barley Woman; the Poles their Baba. In some regions the woman who bound the final sheaf was herself the Baba. She too received a soaking on the way home. Elsewhere Baba was crowned the Harvest Queen, pelted with unripe apples and drenched with water, a signal for the evening's merrymaking to begin. 'Harvest Home! Harvest Home! We've ploughed, we've sowed; We've reaped, we've mowed; And brought safe home, Every load.'

In Celtic regions there was a race to snatch the harvest doll – the Old Hag or *cailleac* – from the harvester as he bore it back to the village. Whoever held the cailleac would feed his plough horse with new grain and old from the cailleac before he cut his first furrow in spring. Some communities were ambiguous about the cailleac; after all, the man who cut the last sheaf was clearly a slow harvester, and a few idle Hebrideans, for example, might wake to find the shaming cailleac mockingly placed in the field of their croft.

Spring was equally important in field legends. On Shrove Tuesday or Mardi Gras (Fat Tuesday), eating pancakes was said to prevent the new grain rotting in the ground. In Bulgaria, Plough Monday preceded Shrove Tuesday, but plough-ing could not begin until a cake had been baked with a coin inside and divided up among the villagers. The one who received the coin was especially blessed. In other countries Plough Monday was earlier in the year, specifically the first Monday after Twelfth Day (the twelfth day after Christmas). This heralded the end of the farm labourer's holiday and was celebrated by drawing a plough through the village and soliciting money for a village shindig. Candles or plough lights were once lit in church, but banned later as a pagan practice.

Harvest home and seed sowing happened at different times of the year in different parts of the world, yet still the rituals continued. The festival of the South American Mataco and Choroti Indians centred around the *algarroba* or

WILD POPPY

Name: Corn poppy, field poppy, Flanders poppy or red poppy (*Papaver rhoeas*)

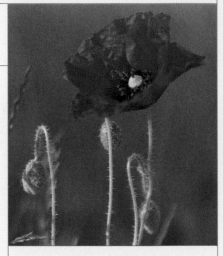

What it's like: Not to be confused with the opium poppy (*Papaver somniferum*), which is an erect, bluey-green and almost hairless annual with white, pink or purple flowers, the wild poppy is a shorter, coarsely haired annual plant. But there is no mistaking the nodding red flower heads of the wild poppy, also known as the corn-rose, or of its habit of flowering profusely on new, broken ground – especially on battlefields, which associated the flower with the blood of the dead. The poppy is imbued with myth and legend. The gods were said to have taken pity on Ceres as she searched desperately for Proserpine, and caused poppies to spring from her footsteps. When she paused to pick one it caused her to sleep and rest at last.

One 16th-century physician from Padua, Italy, advocated the use of poppy seeds to make hens lay more eggs. And if you place a poppy petal over the top of your left fist and clap down on it with your right you know your love is true as long as the poppy petal pops.

Nicholas Culpeper complained that the poppy 'is plentiful enough, and many time too much in the corn-fields' but herbicides have all but eradicated the poppy from the cultivated field.

Where it's grown: Throughout Europe, Asia Minor, northern Africa; naturalised in North America, Australia and New Zealand. Poppies have particular significance within the nations of the British Commonwealth, and artificial ones are distributed as part of the commemorations of Armistice Day at the conclusion of the First World War.

mesquite harvest; in Lithuania it was the rye harvest. For the American Iroquois, whose women performed ritual shuffle dances in homage to the food spirits, there were celebrations for the strawberry, raspberry, beans, green corn and ripe corn crops – and corn legends were deeply entrenched.

One story tells of a Native American who grew tired of digging for roots and lay dreaming in the field. Suddenly he became aware of a beautiful woman with long, light hair standing nearby. She spoke, telling him that, if he were to do as she instructed, she would stay with him forever. She showed him how to make fire, rubbing two sticks together in a clump of dry grass. 'When the sun sets', she told him, 'drag me by my hair over the burned ground.' For, wherever he dragged her, a grass-like plant would spring up, with hair like her own, and feed his people. She was the goddess of corn.

Corn appears too in the Hiawatha legend. A brave was on a fast, worrying over how to feed his people, when on the fourth day Mondamin appeared before him, promising that if they wrestled for three successive evenings, and Hiawatha triumphed, Mondamin would present the brave with an answer to his prayers. Hiawatha, despite being weak from hunger, defeated and killed Mondamin. Burying his opponent, he watched over the spot until a new plant rose from the burial place. It was, of course, corn.

Field Superstitions

The mistletoe was known as 'allheal' for its prodigious health-giving powers. But in Switzerland it was believed the plant must not be cut from the field tree, but knocked, or shot, down from the branches and caught as it fell. Only then could it provide a sure cure for many childhood diseases. In Sweden they believed that the best divining rod for finding water underground was the mistletoe. While it was traditional to kiss beneath a branch of mistletoe hung above the threshold at Christmas, it was equally important to take the plant down and burn it on Twelfth Night if those who had kissed beneath it were ever to marry.

The threshold, and the house and barn doors, were the focus for many superstitions. Creating a new door was a dangerous activity: in some part of Africa it could even cause a family death. Carrying a bride across the threshold, or upending an old horseshoe and fastening it over the barn or house door, are familiar superstitions: but it was also important to leave all the doors open when someone was having a child (to quicken the birth), or dying (to aid the soul's progress). In places as far apart as Finland and the Adriatic, smearing a doorpost with honey protected those beyond the door. Festooning a doorway with may blossom, birch, or a bough broken from a rowan tree helped keep the witches at bay. The Victorian diarist the Reverend Francis Kilvert kept journals during his short life as a clergyman on the Welsh borders. Most were destroyed after his death – possibly because of their salacious content – but this entry survives: 'This evening being May Eve I ought to have put some birch and wittan (mountain ash) over the door to keep out the old witch.' He crossed his fingers that the old witch did not come during the night, although, he wrote, the young witches 'are welcome'. There were witch posts, a lintel or a beam marked with a special sign of St. Anthony to fend off evil spirits or keep the farmhouse safe from lightning. House leeks (*Sempervivum tectorum*) planted on the roof, or a walnut heated on the fire on Easter Sunday, were also said to keep away lightning.

Sometimes a small sheaf of wheat, which had been presented to the farmer by his most senior reaper, was placed over the fireplace for harvest luck. Similarly, a rush that had been blessed on Palm Sunday, or in parts of Europe twigs of box or willow, also helped the harvest along. The vagaries of the harvest were attended by all kinds of superstitions: giving alms or gifts of wheat to the poor was believed to aid the crop. If a stranger happened to pass during harvest it was auspicious to invite them into the field. In France the stranger had to be presented with a nosegay, a bunch of wild flowers. Field flowers, too, were used to decorate the final wagon of wheat as it headed for the harvest home.

In the modern wheat field dropped grains lie where they fall, to be killed off with a herbicide before the next season's crop is planted, but in the past the act of gleaning, collecting the fallen grains, was propitious – although in the region of Arras, France, the women gleaned under the watchful eye of the *garde champêtre*, the village policeman.

There were more rituals to be performed when the wheat was threshed in the autumn. Gifts of sheaves were made to the parish, the wheat auctioned to provide funds for village improvements. In some parts of France an attractive local girl was chosen to be crowned the *Marie au Blé*, the corn bride whose health had then to be toasted at every café in the village. It was also good luck to exchange for a glass or two of wine a sheaf of wheat that the publican would hang on the wall or over the tavern door until the next year's harvest.

The full moon nearest the autumn equinox in the Northern Hemisphere, often a fulsome, blood-red apparition when it rose above the horizon, was known as the harvest moon. But pointing at the moon could cause bad luck, and ignoring the moon's quarters when planting seed was to court failure. John Worlidge in his *Systema Agriculturae* (1669) insisted that turnips or onions, for example, sown when the moon was full, would not 'bulb out', but send up flower stalks instead. The French author Jean-Baptiste de la Quintinye dismissed planting by the moon as bunkum: 'After a diligent observation of the moon's changes for thirty years together ... I perceived that it was no weightier than old wives' tales. Sow what sorts of grains you please, and plant as you please, in any quarter of the moon, I'll answer for your success', he wrote.

There were plenty of superstitions when it came to the rice crop. In some communities, women were forbidden to even approach the crop during menstruation – similar superstitions attended the business of salting the slaughtered pig for winter in Europe. In Sri Lanka the local astrologer would advise on the most propitious colours for the rice planter to wear to ensure a good crop. For good measure a flower was placed over the first seed. If the crop ran into trouble from a drought or a plague of insects, the overseeing goddess, Pattini, could sometimes be pacified by holding a ceremonial coconut fight. Even after the harvest the rice was vulnerable and could be contaminated by someone who had carelessly eaten pork or oily fish (and was therefore unclean) or by a passer-by who swore. Rice wine, *sake*, was an essential part of the rice rituals too: during their New Year celebrations the Japanese supped on sake and rice cakes. As they say in Italy: 'Rice is born in water ... but dies in wine.'

There were yet more superstitions concerning farm animals: the bullfight is a relic from the days when the blood of the sacrificial bull was believed to bring fertility to the ground on which it was spilt. The use of a bull roarer, a piece of bone, stone or wood, which, when whipped through the air on a length of cord, produced a bull-like roar, played its part in rituals from Australia and New Guinea to those of the Pomo Indians of California.

'This evening being May Eve I ought to have put some birch and wittan (mountain ash) over the door to keep out the old witch.'

From the diary of Rev. Francis Kilvert, 1840–79

And what of good fortune? Everyone, including the field worker, needed good luck. In North America it came down to carrying a buckeye or a horse chestnut in your pocket; in Georgia U.S. it helped to blow a kiss at a passing buzzard (turkey vulture). In northern Europe, a cash token, luck money, is still sometimes paid to the buyer of a beast by its seller. Good fortune attended anyone who slept and dreamed of a horse, while in Oldenburg, Germany, good luck was guaranteed if you could pass the first butterfly of the season through the sleeve of your jacket.

Field Sayings

The field means different things to different people. In the Egyptian Osirian religion the afterworld was the Field of Reeds that lay, bathed in perpetual springtime and ruled by Osiris, just beneath the horizon. The Elysian Fields represented paradise or the Fields of the Blessed for the ancient Greeks, while for Parisians the Elysian Fields are the Champs Élysées, the city's central thoroughfare where French traffic creates anything but a sense of peace.

The Field of Blood was the battlefield where the Romans were defeated by Hannibal in 216 B.C.E. and also Aceldama, the field bought by the priests with the 30 pieces of silver that the shame-faced Judas returned to them after betraying Jesus. Accordingly a 'potter's field' was a burial ground reserved for strangers and the poor with no friends.

There was the Field of the Cloth of Gold, the plain in Picardy, France, near Guînes and Ardres where Francis I of France met the English King Henry VIII in June 1520 and where a lavish, temporary palace was built for their negotiations. (Francis had been hoping to enlist Henry as an ally against Charles V, the Holy Roman Emperor: Henry, instead, later made a treaty with Charles.)

There were the curiously named Cold Bath Fields of Clerkenwell, London, established in 1697 to treat rheumatism and other disorders, and the 'three-field system', the crop-rotation method that had survived from the end of the open-field system in England until the reign of King George III and consisted of wheat or rye, followed by peas, beans, barley or oats, and finally by a fallow season.

Everyone likes to make hay while the sun shines, but an event that happened 'between hay and grass' was too late for one thing and too soon for another. A lad who was 'neither hay nor grass' was an adolescent between childhood and adulthood, while a 'hayseed' was a rustic. Behaving in an unruly way or going

SUNFLOWER

Name: Sunflower
(*Helianthus annuus*)

What it's like: This tall plant with a heliotropic flowering head (this habit of following the sun earned it its French name *tournesol*) was used by native North Americans to produce bright black, blue and red dyes for textiles and body paint.

The flower that inspired Vincent van Gogh has been used to make flour, medicines, baskets, paper, buoyancy aids, sweets, cut flowers with low pollen release, health foods and bird feed. In Bavaria, Germany, in 1779 another use for the sunflower was discovered: vegetable oil. Now 90 per cent of sunflowers are grown for oil.

A member of the daisy family, the sunflower grew wild in the southwest of North America (Pueblo Indians used it to treat snake bites and heal wounds).

Although the stems and leaves have their uses, the flower head is the most important part of the plant. It is composed of two types of flower, the outer yellow ray florets and the inner black disc florets, which develop into the sunflower seeds that yield oils with the healthy low-saturated, fatty acid content.

In the mid-20th century Russian plant growers bred flower heads up to 30 centimetres (1 foot) across to increase sunflower oil production by 50 per cent.

Where it's grown: Native to the Americas, the sunflower is now grown commercially in all countries with a temperate climate. It is grown in especially large numbers in Argentina, the United States, France, China, Eastern Europe and Russia.

'haywire' derives from the difficulty of handling the coils of wire used to bind hay when haymaking was first mechanised. Searching for a needle in a haystack or a bottle of hay ('bottle' from the French *botte*, or bundle) is a hopeless undertaking. Similarly, 'ploughing the sands' meant to engage in wasted effort. 'God speed the plough', meaning good luck with your endeavours, may still have some resonance, but ploughing expressions that once peppered country conversations have been mostly forgotten: to 'plough with another man's heifer' was to use information deceitfully gathered; to 'put your hand to the plough' was to begin a serious undertaking; and to 'put the plough before the ox' was to carry out a task back to front, or in the wrong order.

'Up corn, down horn' was more obscure and referred to the usual state of farm economics: when corn or grain was expensive, horn, or beef, became cheaper because people had less money to spend on meat.

When the Cows Lie Down

'When two Englishmen meet, their first talk is of the weather,' wrote Samuel Johnson in 1758. When it comes to the field, subject to sunshine and snow, hail and thunder, fog and low cloud, rain and wind, hurricane and tornado, predicting the weather is uppermost on everyone's mind. Those who spend their working lives in the field develop a feel for weather forecasting. Some experience tension or headaches before a thunderstorm or find that impending wet weather triggers rheumatic pain. Country people also consulted the natural world for weather signs. There was the scarlet pimpernel (*Anagallis arvensis*), otherwise known as the poor man's weatherglass due to its habit of closing its red flowers when rain threatens. The Missouri farmer knew it was time to plant the corn when the first katydid (a long-horned insect related to the grasshopper) appeared while further north, the katydid's arrival meant there were no more than six weeks to the first frost. A halo around the moon meant rain. If there were four stars within the ring then it would rain for four days, or in some cases that rain would fall after four days. More than five stars meant cold weather on the way, or, in some cultures, the number of friends who were soon to die. Weather signs were all a matter of interpretation.

When cows lay down in the field, or seagulls headed for land, wet weather was on the way: 'Seagull, seagull, sit on the sand; It's never fine weather when you're on the land.' A rainbow, or a red sky, in the morning gave the shepherd warning; a rainbow or a red sky at night gave him delight. The farmer could read the clouds: 'Mackerel sky and mares' tails Make lofty ships to carry low sails.'

The amateur forecaster could look to the seasons to gauge the weather to come: 'March winds and April showers Bring forth May flowers.' The expression 'cast ne'er a clout 'til may is out' referred not to the month, but to the blossom of the may tree, or hawthorn, while a heavy crop of berries, or haws, in the autumn was said to signal a hard winter to come.

People have struggled to predict the weather for as long as they have worked in the field. More than 3,000 years ago the Chinese, basing their knowledge on weather observation, divided the calendar into twelve months and further subdivided it into six 'festivals' to aid the farmer: so the summer calendar read 'beginning of summer, grain filling a little, grain in ear, summer solstice, slight heat, great heat.' Muslim scientists and philosophers developed their own detailed weather predictions based on astrological observation, and for centuries the farmer relied on a combination of mythology, astrology and the wind for his weather forecast. Winds were known to bear good and bad weather from Babylonian times. There is the mistral of southern France, the Adriatic *bora*, the Mediterranean *gregale* and the *sirocco*, the North African *khamsin*, and Western Australia's Freemantle Doctor, an afternoon sea breeze that cools Perth down during the summer. Meanwhile, few village churches were built in northern Europe without a weathervane.

The introduction of the barometer brought a touch of science to the business of forecasting, especially after Otto von Guericke, using his barometer, managed to predict a severe storm at Magdeburg in Prussia in 1660 two hours before it struck. The importance of keeping detailed weather records in order to anticipate future weather systems was better understood by 1663 when the Englishman Robert Hooke proposed *A Method for Making a History of the Weather*.

From 1732 the American scientist and statesman Benjamin Franklin was among the first to appreciate the possibility of long-range weather forecasting. He offered such forecasts in his profitable publication *Poor Richard's Almanac*.

'Mackerel sky and mares' tails Make lofty ships to carry low sails.'

R. Inwards, *Weather Lore: A Collection of Proverbs, Sayings, and Rules Concerning the Weather*, 1869

Franklin conjectured that America's severe winter of 1783–4 had been caused by volcanic dust clouds that had been thrown up the previous summer and drifted across the planet to obscure the sun. It would be over a century before he was proved right.

In England in 1777 the Reverend Gilbert White, writing his *Natural History of Selborne* (1789), noted from his weather records how the occurrence the previous spring of 'many summer coincidences' had brought an old tortoise to 'come forth from its dormitory', caused bee swarms and the early arrival of house swallows. When cold weather closed in, the bees, tortoise and swallows retreated – from which, Rev. White concluded, inaccurately, that the swallows must be hibernating. Accuracy, clearly, was still a problem.

The breakthrough in meteorology arrived with Samuel Morse's invention of telegraphy. Franklin and others, including Edmund Halley who had produced a map of the world's winds in the 18th century, realised that weather systems moved on the winds. It followed that if a weather observatory was built upwind of a weather system, it could relay warnings of the weather's approach to those downwind.

Countries such as France began setting up networks of meteorological observation stations connected by telegraph wires, and by the 1860s the Paris Observatory was able to publish daily weather reports. By the 1870s the Observatory was not only providing the best weather warnings in Europe, but also predicting weather patterns in Africa and America.

Today the most accurate weather warnings come from a combination of computer power and satellites. Yet there are those who still look to the farm cat to tell them what the weather holds. A cat that sits with its back to the fire foretells frost on the way. The cat that spends a long time washing its ears and face predicts that the weather has rain in store.

Mysterious Fields

Geometric shapes cut in crops were documented in England as long ago as the 17th century – the phenomenon of the crop circle had arrived. Then, in the late 20th century, the more publicity that these strange circles received, the more they increased in number and complexity. Crop circles have appeared in winter kale crops and rice paddy fields, in nettle beds and even the snow fields of Afghanistan. With over 12,000 reported from Russia and Japan to France and North America, the most numerous and complex were to be found in England, especially close to ancient archaeological sites such as Stonehenge in Wiltshire. Compasses consulted at crop circles are said to develop a mad mind of their own, while mobile phones mysteriously lose their battery power.

Some argued that the self-confessed corn-circle constructors, who, armed with strings, ropes and boards would slip out at night to create ever more eye-catching patterns, were solely responsible. Others looked for paranormal explanations, suggesting that the corn circles were symbols of sacred geometry and the work of civilisations from other planets.

However, the still unresolved mystery of the crop circle is nothing compared to the phenomenon of the birth of farming all those years ago. Now, 10,000 years later, the field struggles to feed the world's 6.7 billion people, but at a cost to the planet: soil erosion and compaction; desertification and over-grazing; the expenditure of non-renewable fossil fuels to grow renewable fuel; famines brought on by dependence on a few staple foods; and international crises such as avian flu and Creutzfeldt–Jakob disease possibly caused by poor husbandry.

Will the fields of the future have to expand and grow yet more efficient crops to feed the world? Or could there be a green transformation, a new agricultural revolution, on the horizon? Will the field continue to use too many chemicals, too much fossil fuel and too much water? Or will the fields of the future yield crops that are more sustainable, more varied, more localised, more environmentally friendly and more productive?

Such a scenario was thought impossible in the 19th and much of the 20th centuries with the rise of the, largely Western, assumption that bigger is better and that small is somehow tribal, inefficient and even inferior.

However, from the writing of the influential intellectual Franz Boas, founder of modern cultural anthropology, who argued that 'The mental attitude of individuals who … develop the beliefs of a tribe is exactly that of the civilised philosopher', to the environmental author E. F. Schumacher, who espoused the cause that 'small is beautiful', it could be that the little family paddy field in Baluchistan will one day prove as environmentally productive as a similar square of land, efficiently cropped and harvested in some former prairie corn belt.

Glossary

Cereal an edible grain such as wheat, rye, oats, maize (corn).

Drowner one who manages water meadows, also called a waterman.

Dust Bowl the consequence of over-farming cereal crops on prairie land leading to dust storms and severe erosion. The most famous instance was in 1930s America.

Enclosures the process of dividing up farmland from open field systems into hedged or fenced fields. Specifically in England during the late 1700s.

Fallow ground that has been ploughed and harrowed but otherwise left uncultivated for a year.

Fenland a low-lying area of eastern England comparable to Dutch polders.

Genetic modification the proces of manipulating an organism's genes in order to produce improvements; in the case of plants these normally take the form of higher yields or resistance to disease.

Irrigation an artificial watering system.

Kibbutzim Israeli communities founded on communal principles.

Milpa the Spanish-Mexican term for a field; used to describe a sustainable crop-growing system that uses no artificial pesticides or fertilisers.

Paddy fields fields that are deliberately flooded in order to grow rice.

Pastoralism relating to shepherds and their flocks; also the depiction of idealised rural life within the arts.

Plantation a large estate upon which a single crop is grown intensively.

Polder low-lying land that has been reclaimed from the sea or a river, especially in the Netherlands.

Prairie temperate grasslands that experience moderate rainfall. The Pampas of South America are one famous example.

Runrig the joint occupation of agricultural land that has been separated into strips, especially in Ireland and Scotland; also called rundale.

Salination the contamination of natural waters such as wells and springs by ground salts.

Slash and burn system of land management involving the raising of crops on ground cleared by cutting down and burning the indigenous bush.

Steppes grassy plains devoid of tree cover especially in southeastern Europe and South West Asia.

Transhumance the seasonal movement of livestock and people from one region to another.

Water meadow a field that lies close to a river and is subject to regular but controlled inundations.

Bibliography

Alderton, David, *The World Encyclopaedia of Birds and Birdwatching*, Lorenz Books, London, 2002

Arthus-Bertrand, Yann, *The Earth from the Air*, Thames & Hudson, London,1999

Arthus-Bertrand, Yann and Michelet, Claude, *Good Breeding*, Harry N. Abrams, New York, 2003

Brown, Jonathan, *Farm Machinery 1750–1945*, Batsford, London, 1989

Bultitude, John, *Apples*, Macmillan, London, 1983

Burton, Maurice, *Meadows and the Forest Margin*, Nelson Doubleday, New York, 1965

Campbell-Culver, Maggie, *The Origins of Plants*, Headline, London, 2001

Darwin, Francis, *The Life and Letters of Charles Darwin*, John Murray, London,1887

Diamond, Jared, *Guns, Germs and Steel: A Short History of Everybody for the Last 13,000 Years*, Norton, New York, 1997

DiSilvestro, Roger, *Audubon: Natural Priorities*, Turner Publishing, Atlanta, Georgia, 1994

Ebrey, Patricia Buckley, *China: Cambridge Illustrated History*, Cambridge University Press, Cambridge, 1996

Firth, Lisa (series ed.), *A Genetically Modified Future?*, Vol. 138, Independence Educational Publishers, Cambridge, 2007

Frost, Louise and Griffiths, Alistair, *Plants of Eden*, Alison Hodge, Penzance, 2001

Furtado, Peter (ed.), *Depression and Dictatorship, History of the 20th Century, Vol. 4 1929–1939*, Hamlyn, London, 1993

Gascoigne, John, *The Enlightenment and the Origins of European Australia*, Cambridge University Press, Cambridge, 2008

Greenoak, Francesca, *Wild Flowers*, Macdonald Guidelines, London, 1977

Hall, Stephen J. G. and Clutton-Brock, Juliet, *Two Hundred Years of British Farm Livestock*, British Museum (Natural History), London, 1989

Hanes, W. Travis III and Sanello, Frank, *The Opium Wars*, Robson Books, London, 2003

Harris, Nathaniel, *The Life and Works of Gustav Klimt*, Parragon, London, 1994

Heath-Agnew, E., *A History of Hereford Cattle and Their Breeders*, Duckworth, London, 1983

Hibberd, Shirley, *Profitable Gardening*, Groombridge & Son, London, 1863

Hobhouse, Henry, *Seeds of Change*, Pan, London, 1985

Huxley, Anthony, *Green Inheritance*, Gaia Books, London, 2005

Kilvert, Francis, *Kilvert's Diary 1870–1879*, Century Publishing, London,1986

Laws, Bill, *Irish Country Style*, Aurum Press, London, 1999

Leach, Marie (ed.), *Funk and Wagnalls Standard Dictionary of Folklore, Mythology and Legend*, Harper, New York, 1972

Leakey, Richard E., *The Making of Mankind*, Book Club Associates, London, 1981

Lucie-Smith, Edward, *American Realism*, Thames & Hudson, London, 1994

Mabey, Richard and Evans, Tony, *The Flowering of Britain*, Hutchinson, London, 1980

Mattison, Chris, *Encyclopaedia of Reptiles and Amphibians*, Grange Books, Kent, 2005

More, Daphne, *The Bee Book*, David & Charles, Newton Abbot, 1976

Musgrave, Toby and Musgrave, Will, *An Empire of Plants*, Cassell, London, 2000

Opie, Iona Archibald and Opie, Peter, *The Oxford Dictionary of Nursery Rhymes*, Clarendon Pres, Oxford, 1951

Porter, Valerie, *Pigs: A Handbook to the Breeds of the World*, Helm, Robertsbridge, 1993

Rackham, Oliver, *The History of the Countryside*, J. M. Dent, London, 1986

Sharkey, Olive, *Common Knowledge*, McPhee Gribble Publishers, Melbourne, 1988

Streeter, David and Richardson, Rosamond, *Discovering Hedgerows*, BBC, London,1982

Vaughan, J. G. and Geissler, C., *The New Oxford Book of Food Plants*, Oxford University Press, Oxford, 1997

Watson, Lyall, *The Whole Hog*, Profile Books, London, 2004

Weather Book, The, Michael Joseph, London, 1982

White, Gilbert, *The Natural History of Selbourne*, Cassell and Company, London, 1846

Wodehouse, P. G., *A Pelican at Blandings*, Arrow Books, London, 2008

Woodell, S. R. J. (ed.), *The English Landscape: Past, Present and Future* (Wolfson College Lectures, 1983), Oxford University Press, Oxford, 1985

Index

HarperCollins Publishers
77-85 Fulham Palace Road
London W6 8JB

www.harpercollins.co.uk

First published in 2010

Quid Publishing
Level 4, Sheridan House
114 Western Road
Hove BN3 1DD
England
www.quidpublishing.com

15 14 13 12 11 10
10 9 8 7 6 5 4 3 2 1

ISBN 978 0 00 735819 9